"Classically, the path to God has been threefold, seeking God in the true, the good, and the beautiful. It is the third way that is the most neglected by contemporary theology, especially by moral theologians. In this book, Pat McCormick offers his insightful take on the moral life via the way of beauty, illuminating a creative and distinctive path for ethical reflection. McCormick is a scholar of substance who writes with flair."

> — Kenneth R. Himes, OFM
> Boston College
> Co-editor of *Modern Catholic Social Teaching:*
> *Commentaries and Interpretations*

"This book is a fine introduction to the often overlooked but powerful role beauty plays in evoking and sustaining the work of justice. Noting that the moral life consists of far more than the minimal obligations we may feel duty bound to fulfill, McCormick explores how it is that the gracious experience of beauty can decenter us. His vivid portrayals of how God is drawing all the world toward the peaceful pleasures of life together enable the reader to feel the pull of beauty toward what is good. This book delineates how it is that this vision of treasured community sparks in those who enjoy it a deep moral desire for the welfare of all, delight in human diversity, and pleasure in the care of creation. Many compelling illustrations drawn from Scripture, literature, art, film, and history bring flesh to McCormick's claims."

> — Patricia Beattie Jung
> Saint Paul School of Theology

"*God's Beauty* is a breakthrough book. McCormick's creativity moves us from the drudgery of duty and obligation to show us the joy and liberation that emerges when we let beauty ground our ethics. The book creatively mines the Scriptures and tradition to discover God as the lure of beauty who transforms how we experience justice, poverty, immigrants, and our world. It's a breath of fresh air for those interested in ethics."

> — Thomas A. Shannon
> Co-editor of *Catholic Social Thought:*
> *The Documentary Heritage*

God's Beauty

A Call to Justice

Patrick T. McCormick

A Michael Glazier Book

LITURGICAL PRESS
Collegeville, Minnesota

www.litpress.org

A Michael Glazier Book published by Liturgical Press

Cover design: Jodi Hendrickson. Cover image: Thinkstock.

Scripture texts in this work are taken from the *Revised English Bible with the Apocrypha* © 1989 by Oxford University Press and Cambridge University Press.

1   2   3   4   5   6   7   8   9

Library of Congress Cataloging-in-Publication Data

McCormick, Patrick T.
    God's beauty : a call to justice / Patrick T. McCormick.
        p.   cm.
    "A Michael Glazier book."
    Includes index.
    ISBN 978-0-8146-8062-9 — ISBN 978-0-8146-8087-2 (e-book)
    1. Social justice—Religious aspects—Christianity.   2. Christianity and justice.   3. Aesthetics—Religious aspects—Christianity.   4. Christian ethics. I. Title.

BR115.J8M39   2012
241'.622--dc23

                                                              2012014321

To my siblings,
Teri, Kitty, Kevin, Mary, Peggy, Betsy, and Ann

Contents

Introduction

Beauty as the Font of Christian Ethics

What if we were to begin our study of Christian ethics not with an examination of our moral duties or the ethical principles that should guide our personal and communal lives, but with an exploration of the call of beauty? Such an approach will strike many as quite strange, perhaps even silly. And yet, beauty, like justice, also draws us outside ourselves, inviting us to attend to, marvel at, and perhaps even begin to care about the object of our attraction and budding affection. In this way beauty generates something of a vocation to a larger, more generous—or at least less self-interested—self. By nurturing our souls with a deep contemplative rest and summoning us to marvel joyfully at the wonder of the other and of all creation, beauty can open our hearts to creature, neighbor, and stranger alike.

If beauty were the starting point of our ethics, we might begin by exploring how it is that the beauty of the righteous community attracts, summons, and encourages us to work for justice and peace. For there is a beauty in communities shot through with justice—a beauty seen in the harmony, balance, and diversity of these societies, in the joy, peace, compassion, and mercy of their members, and in their radiant health, energetic and coordinated creativity, and lively participation—and this beauty somehow attracts, touches, and motivates us. In some way the peaceful and just community is a radiant and wondrous sacrament, a light on a hilltop manifesting and communicating the glory and grandeur of God and summoning and inspiring us to embrace and practice peace and justice. And we are drawn by the beauty of such communities to imitate and improve upon their justice by reforming our own societies, by seeking to make them more just and hence more beautiful.

An ethics that begins with beauty might also wonder why it is that beauty is so critical to us as individuals, why we seem to need beauty as much as we need bread and shelter. For the truth is that persons and communities everywhere have always struggled to carve out some measure of beauty for themselves and their children, and the desire to create some smattering of beauty wells up in every society and human heart. What fundamental need and right do all of us, especially the poor, have to experience and create beauty in our lives and communities? Why are we so impoverished when our lives are stripped of all beauty and so enriched when we find a way to savor and add to the beauty of the world? Why do we need to find or fashion some small scrap of beauty in our lives to feel human or whole? How does beauty touch and awaken something in creatures made in the image and likeness of the Creator of all beauty; and why do we need to experience and add to this beauty to feed our very souls?

And what, then, should we say about the beauty of the other? Why is it also essential to our own humanity that we recognize and treasure the beauty of the stranger, alien, and even the foe and resist every effort to render these unrecognized neighbors ugly? Why are the forces of inhumanity so deeply committed to stripping the other and the stranger of every vestige of beauty, of submerging the beauty of these unrecognized neighbors in a sea of filth and ugliness? And what is the cost to us when we mar or disfigure the face of the stranger, when we turn them into something foul and inhuman? How is it that we become more fully human by recognizing and responding to the beauty of the other?

Finally, in an ethics attending to beauty we might ask what it means in a world increasingly disfigured and degraded by human activity and dominion to say that we have been created in the image and likeness of an artist and gardener who has fashioned the masterpiece of creation and formed us to tend and care for all its beauty. How are we—as works of beauty—called to tend and preserve the beauty of all creation? What is there in us that drives us to protect and cultivate beauty in the world, a beauty that enriches all creatures? And how is it that we are diminished when we turn away from or scorn this beauty?

❖   ❖   ❖

This small work in Christian ethics explores and suggests a number of links between beauty and justice, arguing that beauty is often a path that leads to justice and that real justice is characterized by the harmony, clarity, and balance long associated with beauty. Instead of being a mere distraction, the attraction of beauty can draw us beyond a narrow self-absorption, opening us to the wonder, mystery, and goodness of the other and of the larger world around us and stimulating a generous (or artistic) creativity eager to collaborate with others in building up the masterpiece of the common good. More than a luxury, the enjoyment and creation of beauty is a fundamental right of all peoples, as we are fashioned to be cocreators of beauty and we need some element of beauty to survive and flourish as persons and communities. And when we do not recognize and respond to the beauty of the stranger but seek to render this unrecognized neighbor an ugly and monstrous beast fit for abandonment, abuse, and destruction, we commit the worst sort of injustice and violate our own humanity. In a similar fashion, our failure to preserve and protect the beauty and harmony of creation is a violation of our biblical vocation to be cocreators and caretakers and an offense against the poor and against future generations.

This is a book for Christians who know that ethics is more than a matter of fulfilling duties or following principles, who understand that humans are themselves wondrous works of art fashioned in the image and likeness of the Creator of all beauty. It is a book for those who feel a calling to marvel at, celebrate, and add to the beauty of all creation; a book for those who recognize and respond to the beauty of the stranger, the poor, and all other creatures; a book for those who see themselves as called to compose a life celebrating and shot through with God's beauty.

This little book on beauty and justice seeks to offer a fresh, positive approach to moral arguments calling us to work for social justice, recognize the dignity and rights of the poor, overcome hostility and alienation toward strangers and enemies, and take up our responsibilities to care for and protect the environment and all creation. Instead of laying out the harms or wrongs of failing to work for justice, protect human rights, overcome alienation and hostility, or tend to the earth, *God's Beauty: A Call to Justice* focuses on the calling of divine beauty that summons us to be tenders and creators of beauty.

For God's beauty is seen most clearly in the peaceful and harmonious relations of the just and merciful community, and all humans have a fundamental need and right to share in and contribute to that unfolding beauty. At the same time, we experience the beauty of God in a most profound way in the face-to-face encounter with the neighbor, and we realize our vocation as cocreators of beauty in the labor of tending to and enriching the beauty of creation. And each of these four points is examined in one of the book's chapters.

In the first chapter, "The Beauty of Justice," we see how the beauty of the righteous community—the clearest sacrament of God's glory—summons us to work for justice. For while we have often been urged on to justice by terrifying visions of unjust communities or by threats of punishment and damnation, four biblical accounts summon us to embrace justice by serving up visions of the beauty of the righteous community.

In the creation account of the Sabbath community in Genesis 1:1–2:4 the biblical author provides a vision of a beautiful and harmonious universe where humans are fashioned in the image and likeness of the Creator of beauty. In the creation account of the Eden community in Genesis 2:5-25 we are shown a beautiful world and garden where God, creation, and humans live, work, and play in peace and harmony. The accounts and descriptions of the Promised Land in Exodus, Leviticus, and Deuteronomy describe that "most beautiful of all lands" (Ezek 20:6; NIV) where slavery, debt, hunger, and poverty have been eliminated and where balance and harmony have been reintroduced into human relations. And finally, in the gospel descriptions of the reign of God, Jesus lays out a vision of a beautiful and sumptuous banquet where those who have been stripped of beauty and justice are embraced, healed, nurtured, and liberated.

In each of these four accounts the beauty of righteous communities, seen in their harmony, balance, complexity, and diversity, draws us out of ourselves and invites us to join with others in a dance of peace and justice. These "communions of saints" enchant and encourage us to take up our own communal calling to render the world more just and beautiful.

In the second chapter, "A Right to Beauty," we see that the enjoyment and creation of beauty are not luxuries but fundamental human needs and rights—especially for the poor. All persons and communities, particularly the poor, have a right to savor and create beauty, and no one should be forced to live or work without some access to beauty. For the enjoyment of beauty provides a unique and self-transcending rest (not unlike the contemplative rest of the Sabbath) essential to our dignity and development as persons and communities, and no one stripped of such a rest can be truly free. At the same time, as creatures made in the image and likeness of the Creator of all beauty, all humans have a calling to create beauty, and no one can fulfill his or her basic human vocation if deprived of this right. In addition, persons and communities that are stripped of beauty are inevitably stripped of justice and deprived of their liberty and other rights. Finally, the poor, who have created so much of the world's beauty and been deprived of their fair share of creation's bounty, have a special claim to and need for beauty in their lives and communities.

In the third chapter, "The Beautiful Stranger," we note that every person we encounter possesses a wondrous beauty because he or she is made in the image and likeness of God (*imago Dei*) and because he or she is "bone of our bone and flesh of our flesh" (*imago hominis*; cf. Gen 2:23) Still, when we encounter strangers we often fail to see the beauty of these unrecognized neighbors, and we render them ugly and vulgar in a variety of ways so that we can ignore, oppress, or slaughter them like hostile aliens or monstrous beasts. This is the story of the enslavement of Africans, the Holocaust, and the slaughter in Rwanda. It is the story of our inhumanity to one another.

Throughout Scripture the biblical authors summon us to remember and respond to the beauty and shared humanity of all sorts of strangers, aliens, and enemies. As their God loved them when they were strangers and aliens, the Hebrews are to love the stranger in their midst. And as Christ became a stranger and alien, his believers are to love all strangers as they love Christ. Finding and responding to the beauty of the stranger is essential in recognizing and preserving our own shared humanity.

Finally, in the fourth chapter, "Tending Eden's Beauty," we are reminded that all humans have an ecological vocation to protect and foster the beauty of all creation and to resist the temptation to view creation instrumentally and economically as so much private property to be consumed and abused at will. This ecological calling is more urgent in an age when human activity threatens the beauty, integrity, diversity, bounty, and sustainability of all God's creation, and when many still see humans as called or entitled to exercise an imperial and destructive dominion over nature and other creatures.

Both creation accounts in Genesis 1–2 underscore the universal human vocation to be creators and caretakers of beauty, and they provide us with a "land aesthetic" (like the environmentalist Aldo Leopold's) summoning us to (1) recognize and care for the beauty of all creation, (2) see ourselves as part and parcel of the larger masterpiece of creation, and (3) embrace our divine calling as artists and gardeners to tend to and foster the beauty of creation. As creatures fashioned in the image and likeness of the Creator of all beauty and created to tend and care for this beauty, we have at the core of our being a call to preserve and protect the beauty of all creation—and our failure to tend to and protect this beauty mars and disfigures our very humanity.

In these four chapters we explore the ways that God's beauty—manifest in the harmony, balance, and diversity of the just community, the wondrous face of the stranger, the creative passion of every person, and the marvelous glory of creation—calls us to reach outside ourselves and join with others in the creative labor of building just societies, defending the rights of the poor, making peace with the stranger, and protecting the beauty of all creation. We are made in the image and likeness of the Creator of all beauty, and we are summoned to find and fashion that beauty wherever we can.

Chapter 1

The Beauty of Justice:
Four Biblical Visions of the Beautiful
and Righteous Community

Introduction

In his 1985 thriller *Witness* Peter Weir serves up an idyllic picture of an Amish barn raising in which, to paraphrase Psalm 85, beauty and justice seem to kiss. We watch with palpable pleasure as a gathering of neighbors assemble and construct a cathedral-like barn for a newlywed couple; the gracious harmony and coordination of these volunteer carpenters and quilters becomes a gorgeous ballet cast against a sun-drenched backdrop of lush rolling hills. But the beauty of this symphonic labor is also an expression of justice, for in this picture of generous and peaceful collaboration Weir has captured a snapshot of the righteous community, a community in which men and women work (and play) well with one another and are bound together by right relations. And when this gathering of friendly neighbors sits down at their noonday meal to break bread with one another, Weir offers us a banquet that captures both the beauty and the justice of the righteous community.

We do not often think of beauty and justice as playmates, and "the beautiful people" castigated by biblical prophets or covered by gossip columnists are rarely thought of as just or righteous. Still, the righteous community, that society shaped by justice and characterized by a harmonious ordering of all its parts in a free and peaceful collaboration, is a thing of beauty. Like the ballet of Weir's barn raising or the *ronde* in Botticelli's *Allegory of Spring*, the righteous community has the beauty of a joyous and well-choreographed dance. The harmony created by the coordinated labors of a community of people giving and receiving their fair share of the common good, exercising and developing their full range of talents by joining with others in a shared labor and life that is larger than any of them—this is a work of justice and beauty.

And the righteous community (as we will see below) is also a sacrament of God's beauty, for in the harmonious and well-ordered society shot through with peace and justice we have the clearest sacrament of God's glory. Genesis 1 tells us that the creation that reflects the glory and grandeur of its Creator is a symphonic universe of harmonious relations. The chaos and violence of the formless wasteland and murky abyss is replaced by a symmetrical balance of light and dark, sun and moon, and land and sky and sea, as well as a teeming and lavish symphony of creatures who share space and food. This harmonious creation is a splendid and well-apportioned cathedral reflecting in the unity and communion of its various parts the wholeness and beauty of its Creator. Indeed, the humans who are fashioned in the very image and likeness of this Creator (and who must then capture the divine likeness in a special way) are fashioned *as* a community, an interdependent couple of diverse and complimentary parts. The beauty of creation is found in the righteous community, which best reflects the beauty of the Creator.

Like other works of beauty, the righteous community attracts us. Visions of the righteous community do not merely please us; they draw us out of ourselves, inspire us, and call us to reach beyond ourselves and our present arrangements. The beauty of the righteous community has us reaching (beyond our grasp?) for the heaven that is justice. And like any other work of beauty, we wish to copy and imitate the righteous community. Seeing the beauty of the righteous community, we are inspired to fashion other works of art in its image and likeness.

So when Martin Luther King Jr. offers his vision of a righteous America in his "I Have a Dream" speech, we feel the attraction of a society where prejudice, discrimination, and segregation have been replaced by racial harmony, equality, and reconciliation. In King's vision (or dream) the righteous community is a thing of beauty, a land flowing with the milk and honey of compassion, justice, and freedom.

Scripture also offers us beautiful visions of the righteous community, or visions of the community that is both righteous and beautiful. And in these visions the righteous community is beautiful *because* it is just. The harmony established among and between humans, and between humans and the rest of creation and the Creator, is justice, and this justice (or harmony) has the beauty of a great work of art or architecture. It stuns and summons us, awakening within us a deeply rooted passion to become cocreators of such beauty. We are like Renaissance artists moved by the glory of ancient Greece and Rome, or like Beethoven inspired by Mozart. The beauty that captures us wells up within us and must find its own fresh expression.

In the first and second creation accounts of Genesis 1-2, in the visions of the Promised Land found in Exodus, Leviticus, and Deuteronomy, and in Jesus' New Testament vision of the Heavenly Banquet, the Bible presents us with four images of the righteous community, images of breathtaking beauty that draw us out of ourselves and summon us to "go and do likewise." In these visions of the Sabbath, Eden, Canaan, and the reign of God, the righteous community shines forth before us like Hopkins's "shook foil," and, bedazzled, we are charged to transform our own communities into such works of art.

This chapter will explore the ways four biblical visions of the righteous community unveil the beauty of justice and rely on this beauty to summon us to imitate this righteousness and become cocreators of God's justice. We will examine how the first two creation narratives in Genesis 1–2 offer complementary visions of the righteous community, summoning us from violence and isolation to peace and communion; how the vision of a Promised Land flowing with the milk and honey of justice and compassion inspires the Hebrews to fashion a righteous community that will be the most beautiful of lands; and how Jesus' vision of the reign of God as a Heavenly Banquet draws us beyond the injustices of empire toward a community where beauty and justice are one.

But first we will see how beauty and justice might kiss, how beauty, which is so often cast as foe or folly, can be a friend of justice. We will see how justice has a beautiful face and how the righteous community might be called a thing of beauty.

The Analogy of Beauty and Justice

Biblical authors warn that the beauty of adornments and riches are deceptive and ephemeral, and they castigate the greedy and unjust for coveting beautiful mansions and possessions while oppressing and robbing the poor.[1] In this light, beauty seems like a distraction or an obstacle to the pursuit of justice—an attractive siren who will captivate and lead us astray.

But Scripture also speaks of "the beauty of the LORD," which will shine forth from Zion and before which the righteous desire to spend all their days.[2] And biblical authors write as well of a person's real or internal beauty, which consists of one's good character and noble virtues. This is a beauty to be coveted by the just and the righteous—and to be blessed by God. Moreover, as we will see below, Scripture suggests that the righteous or just community is itself a thing of beauty, reflecting as it does God's own beauty and inspiring others to imitate and recreate this harmonious splendor.

Outside the pages of Scripture it has long been recognized that while beauty and justice are not identical, they are analogous; both are achieved by a harmonious ordering of their various parts. As Wladyslaw Tatarkiewicz notes in "The Great Theory of Beauty and Its Decline,"[3] classical definitions of beauty from the Pythagoreans and Plato to Thomas Aquinas and Michelangelo focused on a harmonious arrangement of the various parts of a work of art, architecture, or music. At the same time, philosophers from Plato forward described justice in terms of a harmonious ordering of the community achieved when each part of society contributes and receives its proportionate share. And so, while a great work of beauty may not possess the virtue of justice (and may indeed be the product of a grave injustice), a just or righteous community *does* possess a certain beauty.

Beauty as Harmonious Proportion

According to Tatarkiewicz, the Pythagoreans maintain that "order and proportion are beautiful and fitting"; Plato declares that "the maintenance of measure and proportion is always beautiful" and that "the absence of measure is ugly"; Aristotle asserts that "beauty consists in magnitude and ordered arrangement" and that the main forms of beauty are "order, proportion, and definiteness"; and the Stoics claim that "the

---

[1] See, e.g., Jas 1:11; 1 Pet 3:2-4; Prov 31:29-31; Ps 37:20; Amos 4:1-3; 6:4-6.
[2] See, e.g., Ps 50:2; 27:3-5.
[3] Wladyslaw Tatarkiewicz, "The Great Theory of Beauty and Its Decline," *The Journal of Aesthetics and Art Criticism* 31, no.2 (Winter 1972): 165–80.

beauty of the body resides in the proportion of the limbs in relation to one another and to the whole."[4]

In *Ten Books on Architecture* the Roman architect Vitruvius reports that the attractiveness of a building is achieved "when the appearance of the work is pleasing and elegant, and the proportions of its elements have properly developed principles of symmetry," and he notes that a "work has a masterful beauty because of its symmetries and their harmony."[5] Vitruvius maintains the same was true in sculpture and painting, as well as in nature, "which has created the human body in such a way that the skull from the chin to the upper brow and hairline makes up one tenth of the entire length of the body." In his view it was possible to present the just proportions of both buildings and human bodies in numerical terms.[6]

St. Augustine agrees that beauty was a question of harmonious relations among a work's various parts, arguing that "only beauty pleases; and in beauty, shapes; in shapes, proportions; and in proportions, numbers." Furthermore, he offers "the venerable formulation for beauty: measure, shape, and order."[7] The medieval theologian Pseudo-Dionysius argues in *Divine Names* that beauty consists in "proportion and brilliance," and St. Thomas Aquinas repeats that definition when he writes that beauty consists in integrity, due proportion or harmony, and clarity, and that "the beauty of the body consists in a man having his bodily limbs well proportioned, together with a certain clarity of color."[8] The Renaissance architect Leon Battista Alberti echoes these sentiments when he argues that

> Beauty is that reasoned harmony of all the parts within a body, so that nothing may be added, taken away, or altered, but for the worse. . . . Beauty is a form of sympathy and consonance of the parts within a body, according to definite number, outline, and position, as dictated by *concinnitas*, the absolute and fundamental rule

---

[4] Ibid., 167.

[5] Vitruvius Pollio, *Ten Books on Architecture*, trans. Ingrid D. Rowland (New York: Cambridge University Press, 1999), 26 and 84.

[6] Ibid., 47.

[7] Tatarkiewicz, "The Great Theory of Beauty and Its Decline," 168.

[8] Thomas Aquinas, *Summa Theologica*, trans. the Fathers of the English Dominican Province, first complete American edition, 2 vols (New York: Benziger Brothers, 1947), I, 5, 4, ad 1m; ST I, 39, 8; ST II II, 145, 2.

in nature. This is the main object of the art of building, and the source of her dignity, charm, authority, and worth.[9]

Justice as Harmonious Proportion

In a similar fashion Plato understands justice as that virtue concerned with the harmonious ordering of the whole, achieved by every part doing its task, with nobody encroaching on another's domain or authority. The just person is one who experiences a harmonious ordering of his intellect, emotion, and desire, and the just soul is one that is harmoniously ordered by reason. This internal justice is, for Plato, achieved among the various parts of a person's soul. Meanwhile, a similar harmony is achieved in the larger society when individuals and groups render their proper service and exercise their appropriate authority. This larger social justice is achieved among the citizens of a city or nation. In both cases Plato describes justice as "the quality of everyone doing his own work and not being a busybody."[10]

Indeed, Plato reports that the just person brings his or her three parts (intellect, emotion, and desire) "into harmony, just like three notes on a harmonic scale—lowest, highest, and middle."[11] And he describes a just state as one where its three classes each work in harmony with one another, producing a well-ordered community, while the unjust state is ill-ordered and at war with itself.[12]

Likewise, the Bible describes justice as "fidelity to the demands of a relationship," seeing justice as a matter of right or well-ordered relations with God, neighbor, and the larger community. In the Bible, "laws are just not because they conform to an external norm or constitution, but because they create harmony within the community," and "justice is a harmony which comes from a right relationship to the covenant Lord and to the neighbor to whom a person is related by covenant bond." By the same token, "injustice is not simply a bad moral attitude, but a social cancer which can bring chaos to the goods of the earth."[13]

---

[9] Leon Battista Alberti, *On The Art of Building in Ten Books*, trans. Joseph Rykwert, Neil Leach, and Robert Tavernor (Cambridge, MA: MIT Press, 1991), 156, 303.

[10] Plato, *The Republic*, bk. IV, 433d., in *The Dialogues of Plato*, 4th ed., ed. and trans. B. Jowett (Oxford: Clarendon Press, 1953), 286.

[11] Ibid., bk IV, 443d.

[12] Ibid., bk IV, 435b.

[13] John R. Donahue, SJ, "Biblical Perspectives on Justice," in *The Faith That Does Justice*, ed. John C. Haughey, SJ (New York: Paulist Press, 1977), 71 and 78.

So beauty and justice are both concerned with the harmonious arrangement of the different parts or elements of a work or society, and the just or righteous community has a certain well-ordered beauty to it that creates peace and harmony, while the unjust society is characterized by the chaos of violence and iniquity.

The Attraction of Beauty and Justice

Though this will seem self-evident for beauty, both beauty and justice are attractive. They each draw us out of and beyond ourselves, attracting us like moths to the light, enlarging and—yes—pleasing us.

Along with the harmony and symmetry of beauty, Aquinas notices clarity and color of beauty, hinting perhaps at the sharp, aching beauty of a single rose in the morning light or a patch of mustard yellow on a blue quilt. The beauty that pleases, that stuns and awakens something within us, that leaves us momentarily breathless, also pulls us out of our ruts and routines and draws us into something larger and greater.

But this beauty does not shove. It does not push us from outside like some "should" or "ought." It pulls and draws us, attracting us with pleasure, clarity, and color. Elaine Scarry notes that beauty draws us beyond ourselves, enlarging our soul and point of view. "It is not that we cease to stand at the center of the world, for we never stood there. It is that we cease to stand even at the center of our own world. We willingly cede our ground to the thing that stands before us."[14] Mortimer Adler argues that beauty opens us up to contemplation, providing a self-transcending rest that pulls us beyond ourselves and renders us fully human.[15] We are decentered by beauty, or as Iris Murdoch argues, "unselfed" by beauty.[16] And this unselfing that pulls us beyond the narrow narcissism of our daily routines and self-involved preoccupations is not a burden or penalty but a joy (as Keats would say). Beauty unselfs us with pleasure.

Justice too has its self-transcending appeal. Of the four cardinal virtues, it is justice alone that draws our eye or attention to the other, that is interested in the neighbor, the stranger, the larger community. Temperance, prudence, and courage direct us to protect and attend to ourselves and

---

[14] Elaine Scarry, *On Beauty and Being Just* (Princeton, NJ: Princeton University Press, 1999), 111.

[15] Mortimer J. Adler, *Six Great Ideas* (New York: Macmillan, 1981), 129–30.

[16] Scarry, *On Beauty and Being Just*, 112–13.

our own, but only justice unselfs and decenters us and asks that we look to the needs, rights, and happiness of the world outside. Only justice seeks to render the other his or her due. As Aristotle notes, "Justice, alone of the virtues, is thought to be the good of another, because it . . . does what is of advantage to others." [17]

And, as Scarry notes, there is a beauty or attraction in justice as well. [18] We do not approach the unselfing call of justice as slaves hitched to a yoke. Instead, when justice captures or enflames us, we are touched by a love of the other. Suddenly, we see the stranger, the outcast, or even the enemy *as if* they had the beauty of our own child, sibling, or neighbor. We see their humanity, their holiness, their unique, startling, and concrete appeal. Justice becomes a passion drawing us to the previously unrecognized and overlooked wonder of the one who is other. "Here at last," we cry with the first solitary human, "is bone from my bones, flesh from my flesh!" (Gen 2:23).

At the same time, there is something attractive about the well-ordered and harmonious community, something pleasing in the experience of sharing resources and labor with others—of working and playing well with others. Perhaps that is because, as Genesis 2 reminds us, it is not good for us to be alone. We humans are social creatures meant to be in the harmonious company of others, built to be in relationship with one another—and justice is the well-ordered relationship, the tending to the self that is larger than our little selves.

The Beauty of the Righteous Community: Four Biblical Visions of Beauty and Justice

If beauty unselfs and decenters us with its attractions, so too a vision of justice can offer itself as a thing of beauty that draws us out of ourselves and into harmony with others. Radiant with its own integrity, harmony, and clarity, the dream or vision of the righteous community pulls us beyond the chaos and violence of our disordered communities and draws us to the light of justice. Martin Luther King Jr.'s "I Have a Dream" speech summons his audience to racial justice and harmony by offering a beautiful vision of a land where sisters and brothers of every

---

[17] Aristotle, *Nicomachean Ethics*, trans. and ed. Martin Ostwald (New York: MacMillan Publishing, 1989), bk. V, 1.

[18] Scarry, *On Beauty and Being Just*, 91.

race live in peace with one another. Isaiah summons Israel to justice by offering up a vision of the beauty of a righteous and liberated Jerusalem. And Paul inspires the early Christians to practice justice and compassion to one another by calling them to recognize the glory and beauty of the resurrected Body of Christ of which they are a part.

The beauty of the righteous community is seen in the symmetry and harmonious balance of a society in which all persons and groups receive and contribute their fair share, are treated justly and render justice unto each other, and are allowed to participate fully in the larger group and develop their whole range of talents and gifts. According to Scarry, we "see" the beauty of the righteous community in assemblies and small communities. Paul sees the absence of this justice in the separate and unequal tables at which Corinthian Christians break bread, while we see examples of this beautiful justice in the barn raising in *Witness* and the cafeteria scene in *Fame*, and we see the ugliness of its absence in the Potterville of Capra's *It's a Wonderful Life*.

Scripture offers us (at least) four visions of the beautiful and just community and presents the righteous community as a wonder to behold. In the two creation accounts of Genesis 1–2 we read about God fashioning global and human communities characterized by a wondrous and peaceful harmony that is both just and beautiful. And in the Exodus narrative of Israel's deliverance from Egypt we learn of a Promised Land that is both a thing of beauty and a work of justice. And in the gospels Jesus announces the coming of God's reign, a new and entirely different sort of community that will be like a rich and beautiful banquet in which all the victims of injustice and oppression will finally receive the full and lasting justice of God.

Creation I: Genesis 1:1–2:4
The Creation of the Beautiful and
Righteous (Sabbath) Community

A Beautiful Masterpiece

We are told seven times in Genesis 1:1–2:4 that creation is a work of beauty. On each of the six days on which God labored to bring about the created world, we read that "God *saw* that it was good" (or even "delightful"), and on the last of these days, when looking upon everything he created, "God *saw* that it was *very* good" (and so "exceedingly delightful").[19] This is clearly an aesthetic judgment about creation, both in its individual parts and as a harmonious whole. For, as Aquinas tells us, beauty is that which pleases upon being seen, and God has seen all of creation as good and delightful—rendering the divine Creator well pleased.

The full beauty of creation, however, is seen when "God saw *all* that he had made, and it was *very* good." For, like any great masterpiece, the complete beauty of creation is found not merely in its individual parts but in its overall composition (wholeness, harmony, and proportions). This symphonic work fashioned by God is beautiful in its wholeness, and this beauty is to be found in the way this wholeness manifests the beauty of a triune God, a God who is Community. Not only are humans (male and female) made in the image and likeness of God, who is relational, but all creation in its wholeness reflects the beauty of a God who is triune.

Indeed, the biblical author communicates the beauty of creation by portraying it as the construction of a great architectural masterpiece—a temple or cathedral that opens our hearts and minds to the transcendent (as beauty does) by embodying symmetry, proportion, and harmony. As S. Dean McBride writes, the creation that "takes material shape in response to God's speaking is a palatial abode," which Philo of Alexandria referred to as the highest and holiest temple of God.[20]

McBride goes on to show that the beauty of this temple is revealed in both the structure and the sequence of its design. Architecturally, the ugly chaos of a vast wasteland and murky deep are replaced by a three-tiered structure of water, sky, and land, each with its own proper space and sharply defined boundaries and each resting firmly upon or holding up the others. The hammered dome of the sky is a vaulted ceiling holding back the upper waters of the deep and fixing the lights of the sky in place. The marshy deep below has been drained off to fill the ocean and seas and provide a firm foundation of land on which plants and animals may blossom and flourish. And the clear blue sky between ceiling and crypt teems with all sorts of birds and winged creatures.

---

[19] Richard H. Lowery, "Sabbath and Survival: Abundance and Self-Restraint in a Culture of Excess," *Encounter* 54, no. 2 (Spring 1993): 148; see also Richard H. Lowery, *Sabbath and Jubilee* (St. Louis, MO: Chalice Press, 2000), 86–87.

[20] S. Dean McBride Jr., "Divine Protocol: Genesis 1:1–2:3 as Prologue to the Pentateuch," in *God Who Creates*, ed. William B. Brown and S. Dean McBride Jr. (Grand Rapids, MI: Eerdmans, 2000), 11.

And this same harmonious architectural beauty is seen in the sequence of creation. The six days of God's labor are divided into two sets of three days, with the second half repeating and building upon the labor of the first three days. Building from the sky down (instead of the ground up), God's creation unfolds in three vertical levels in the first three days, and then each of these levels are furnished and outfitted in the second three days. And the seventh day becomes the crown or apse of this great work, completing the masterpiece of creation.[21]

Thus, creation is a sacrament of the Creator, a work of art that embodies and reflects the beauty in the mind of the artist and imitates the one who is Beauty itself. Each individual part and the whole symphonic harmony manifest the beauty of creation's maker.

That creation is a work of beauty is also driven home by the fact that humans and other creatures feel impelled to imitate and continue this labor, joining in the divine labor of creation by being fruitful and multiplying. As Scarry notes, beauty inspires us to make copies, to fashion our own versions, to enter into the creative process.[22] One great work of art inspires another, and another, and another. Beethoven hears Mozart. Caravaggio sees Michelangelo. Beauty begets beauty, which begets more beauty. And humans and other creatures—created by and in the image and likeness of the Creator—take up the work of beauty by filling up the earth with their own works of cocreation.

From Chaos to Cosmos

But we also read in Genesis 1:1–2:4 that creation is a work of justice, for this first creation narrative recounts the construction of a righteous and harmonious community.[23] As we will see, out of a formless wasteland of chaos and violence God fashions a beautiful, bounteous, and organic community in which Creator and creatures live and work in harmony with one another. Indeed, the labor of creation is precisely the fashioning of this just and righteous community in which the integrity of each part and the harmony of all parts is established and built up in an organic work of art. So it is that the very beauty of creation *is* its justice, and the harmony, symmetry, and clarity of this symphonic work of beauty is to

[21] Ibid., 12–13.
[22] Scarry, *On Beauty and Being Just*, 3.
[23] McBride, "Divine Protocol," 3.

be found in the rightly ordered relationships (justice) that tie all creatures to one another and to their Creator.

The creation account in Genesis 1:1–2:4 begins with chaos and desolation (a formless wasteland with darkness hovering over a great abyss) and leads to a well-ordered and harmonious cosmos in which all creation and its creatures come together in a peaceful and just community.

The Hebrew terms describing the primal wildness at the start of this creation story—*tohu wabohu*—point to uncultivated wilderness "full of undomesticated and dangerous beasts that devour crops, raid flocks, and attack humans who wander there."[24] As Richard Lowery writes, "*Tohu wabohu* is the uncontrollable chaos that threatens the social and ecological order. . . . It is [an] unpredictable and unmanageable disaster that breaks without warning and threatens to destroy social life."[25]

Tohu wabohu might also describe a terrain devastated by war and conquest, not unlike the Judean countryside encountered by Jews returning from the Babylonian captivity in 538 BCE (about the time the Priestly author composed this creation narrative). The vast wasteland of *tohu wabohu* could well describe the carnage of ancient Carthage or the more recent annihilation of Dresden or Hiroshima. In both the ancient and the modern worlds the fog of war lays low the work of nature and civilization, destroying environment and infrastructure and leaving behind a wasteland some call "peace."

This is the wasteland and chaos of Picasso's *Guernica*, unveiling the mindless devastation of war, in whose gaping maws towns and countryside are chewed up like sausage. It is the endless murk and mess of trench warfare, described to T. S. Eliot by one soldier as a sea of "mud like porridge, trenches like shallow and sloping cracks in the porridge, porridge that stinks in the sun."[26]

Or perhaps *tohu wabohu* evokes the desolation of a world befouled and exhausted by abuse and disregard, a place where crops no longer grow, where the water is too polluted to support life, where the sky is so thick with smoke and dust that there is no day or night. Ancient and modern

---

[24] Lowery, *Sabbath and Jubilee*, 82.

[25] Ibid., 83.

[26] The quote comes from a soldier's letter Eliot submitted to the British weekly *The Nation* (published June 23, 1917) and republished in *The Sunday Indian* on July 5, 2009. The full text may be found at http://en.wikisource.org/wiki/The_Nation_(UK)/War and http://www.thesundayindian.com/article_print.php?article_id=7709 (accessed on February 15, 2012).

audiences of Genesis would both know of places where humanity's footprint has crushed and exhausted life and creation, leaving a desert or befouled abyss.

In either case, whether the vast wasteland is the fruit of war or environmental degradation, God's creation of the world in Genesis 1:1–2:4 becomes an act of nation or world building, a peacemaking recovery of order, community, and life in which creation is not—as in some other ancient myths—an act of sacred or redemptive violence, but rather the building up of a peaceful and harmonious community.[27] For instead of God fashioning the world by conquering his enemies and using their carcasses as brick and mortar for a new universe, the Creator in Genesis 1:1–2:4 has come to repair the wreckage of violence and abuse and, out of this wasteland of carnage and chaos, to create a temple of peace and justice. The work of creation in Genesis 1:1–2:4 deconstructs the destruction of war and calls humanity to participate in this world-building labor of creating a beautiful and just society.[28]

Genesis 1:1–2:4 is the account of the creation of a sociopolitical unit—of a just and peaceful society.[29] This creation narrative moves from the barren chaos and wasteland of war (or environmental degradation) to the bountiful garden and cosmos of peace or Sabbath. The narrative begins with a world where the fog of war has annihilated the boundary between light and dark, imprisoned us in a timeless hell without day or night, fouled and confused lands and rivers into a porridge of stinking mud, stripped the skies, sea, and land of every form of life, and made humans into beasts and enemies.

Into this wasteland God introduces a creation that gives back our days and nights (and seasons); reconstructs a safe roof over our heads; drains the moors and swamps and irrigates the lands, providing arable and well-watered terrain that can supply shelter and produce a growing bounty of harvests and habitats for all sorts of living creatures; welcomes back flocks of returning birds, schools of fish, and legions of deep-sea creatures, as well as herds of cattle, sheep, and all manner of crawling creatures; and finally provides a safe place for the birthing and raising

---

[27] J. Richard Middleton, "Created in the Image of a Violent God? The Ethical Problem of the Conquest of Chaos in Biblical Creation Texts," *Interpretation* 58, no. 4 (October 2004): 341, 352.

[28] Elaine Scarry, *The Body in Pain: The Making and Unmaking of the World* (New York: Oxford University Press, 1987), 61–63.

[29] McBride, "Divine Protocol," 3, 11–14.

of our children and for the recognition of our neighbors as fellow creatures made in God's image.

And in this world-building labor God fashions a community of creatures who are to share the land and sea and skies with one another, making room for all creatures to find habitats where they may flourish without crowding one another out. The command to be fruitful and multiply is given to both humans (1:28) and other creatures (1:22), implying that all are to have a place in this community and the resources they will need to build their nests and feed their young.

For in this just and harmonious society God is fashioning, all creatures are also to receive a fair portion of food (Gen 1:29-30)—much as the Hebrews in Exodus 16 are each to receive a sufficient portion of manna by learning to share. The world's plants and trees are to be shared by humans and other creatures so that all will have enough to eat—and, of course, all will have to exercise prudence and temperance to ensure that future generations of life will find sufficient food. Thus, humans and other creatures will need to make certain that grasses and seed-bearing plants produce fresh crops.

The culmination of the world-building labor of Genesis 1:1–2:4 is the just and peaceful community of the Sabbath. For the six days of labor lead up to the day on which God rests, the (only) day that God blesses and makes holy. This Sabbath is the masterpiece God has been fashioning, a new day in which the wasteland and abyss of violence and injustice have been replaced by a peaceful and just cosmos, a temple in which peace and justice (and beauty) dwell and kiss.

The day of God's rest (*shabat*), which is the culmination of creation, is a day of beauty and justice. The God who found all the things created in the first six days so pleasing to the eye now blesses and makes holy the completed masterpiece. Like any artist, God stands back to admire and bless the finished work (which the author tells us is complete or finished four times in three verses). This is a moment to bask in the beauty of creation, to savor its completion and perfection, which is so different from the ugly and formless wasteland from which it has been fashioned.

But this seventh day is also a day of justice. For a Sabbath is only possible for people who are free and fed. Slaves and those trapped in crippling debt or poverty can only dream of a day of rest. The Sabbath in Genesis 2:1-4 is a time when all people have been liberated, when every shackle and bond has been loosed, when no one is slave or debtor. On this Sabbath humans are not cursed to toil "*all* the days of your life" (Gen

3:17; emphasis added); rather, they live off a bounty that provides rest. To paraphrase Deuteronomy 15:4, God's labor of creation has culminated in a day when "there will be no poor among you." And so the seventh day points both to the peaceable character of creation and to the liberation of humanity from bondage to slavery and injustice.[30]

A day of rest is also a day of peace, a day when there are no enemies, when no one lays siege to our cities, when our sons and daughters are not dying in battle, and when we do not live in fear of attack. Like the eleventh-century Truce of God, which outlawed war on Sundays, holy days, and certain liturgical seasons, the Sabbath day of rest was a time of peace.[31]

Finally, the day of rest in Genesis 2:1-4 is a day of worship, a day when humans may turn from their toil and contemplate the beauty and wonder of God's creation and its maker. As God pauses to bless and make holy this day, so humans pause to bless God and creation. And this pause, this rest, is a contemplative act that opens humans to the sacred, the transcendent.[32] Such a rest transforms us from slaves and beasts of burden into something just less than angels. The beauty of creation, enjoyed in this moment of rest, can only be savored by persons who are fully human and free. The Sabbath as a day of worship is also a day of justice. And it is a day when we are transformed by the beauty of God and creation.

Genesis 1:1–2:4 offers us a vision of beauty and justice. The world created by God in this account is pleasing to the divine eye and is blessed and made holy. The beauty of this creation is found in its individual parts and its overall symmetry and harmony. The formless wasteland and dark abyss are forged into a well-ordered cosmos filled with a bounteous and teeming variety of life. At the same time, this beautiful world is characterized by justice and peace, and indeed the moral harmony of God's creation is a source of its beauty, just as creation's beauty decenters all creatures and draws them into peaceful and right relations with God and one another.

---

[30] Marsha M. Wilfong, "Human Creation in Canonical Context: Genesis 1:26-31," in *God Who Creates*, ed. William B. Brown and S. Dean McBride Jr., eds. (Grand Rapids, MI: Eerdmans, 2000), 42–52. For ways the creation narrative of Genesis 1:1–2:4 summons us to peace, see Lowery, *Sabbath and Jubilee*, 82–83ff.

[31] Ronald H. Bainton, *Christian Attitudes toward War and Peace* (New York: Abingdon Press, 1960), 110.

[32] Adler, *Six Great Ideas*, 129–30.

Creation II: Genesis 2:4b-25
The Beauty of the Creation of the Garden of Eden

The second creation narrative in Genesis 2 also describes a work of beauty. That Eden is a thing of beauty seems self-evident. It is a paradise. If the vast wasteland and chaos of *tohu wabohu* refer to an uncultivated wilderness "full of undomesticated and dangerous beasts," then the garden God has planted in Eden represents its polar opposite. Unlike a desert or a jungle, which are each hostile and uninhabitable wildernesses, a garden welcomes, sustains, and pleases humans. It is a cultivated oasis in the midst of an uncertain and sometimes unfriendly world. And unlike forests and savannahs, gardens are human artifacts, fashioned and tended by and for humans to provide a retreat or sanctuary, a place of beauty to soothe and nourish the human spirit.

For the modern reader, a garden can also be a respite from the cramped and sometimes desolate terrain of urban landscape, a break from the grays and browns of concrete and smog, a momentary holiday from the rush and blare of traffic. Like stepping into a church or museum, the visitor to a garden seeks a small piece of beauty with which to nourish her soul, a minute of contemplative rest inspired by a single rose or "a host of golden daffodils," as Wordsworth writes.

In both the ancient and the modern worlds' gardens are works of beauty. The hanging (or terraced) gardens of Babylon were considered one of the seven wonders of the ancient world, and the water gardens of Egypt filled the eye with water lilies and lush ornamental grasses. Louis XIV's formal architectural gardens at Versailles have entertained and delighted royals and tourists for over three centuries, while millions of other visitors have found solace and pleasure in the more naturalistic and informal arrangements of English gardens and city parks (like New York's Central Park), and still others seek out the quiet and restrained beauty of Japanese gardens. These are lovely places, grassy temples full of quiet wonder, shady cathedrals lit by a thousand blossoms. Indeed, even botanical gardens, once planted primarily for medical and scientific purposes, now provide a delightful respite for modern city dwellers in search of sweet vistas of ornamental plants and flowering shrubs, and their greenhouses bring lush, tropical blossoms to those of us trapped in winter's grip. There is a reason one sees a thousand brides in these parks and gardens every spring, posing under trellises or in front of lily ponds—and a reason millions of us snip the blossoms from our own gardens to decorate our homes and tables. We know beauty when we see it.

And the garden God plants (and humans tend) in Eden is an especially beautiful masterpiece, for "Eden" refers to a "fertile plain" and is close to the Hebrew word for "delight," so a garden in Eden would be understood as a "garden of delight," a "pleasure park," or a paradise.[33] And if the world fashioned in Genesis 1:1–2:4 is God's temple, this garden in Eden is God's fertile abode, a sweet and lavish dwelling place where God walks with humans in the cool of the evening.

The biblical author describes Eden as a bountiful, well-watered, and lovingly tended garden. In this lush garden God has planted "every kind of tree *pleasing to the eye* and good for food" (Gen 2:9; emphasis added) so that it produces a cornucopia of delights for the eye and palate, satisfying our appetite for beauty and nourishment. And in this idyllic park humans labor without toil or strain, pruning and harvesting Eden's bounty, which is given up to them without sweat, thorns, or thistles.

Indeed, Eden's bounty and beauty overflow its borders, and the river that flows from it and waters its garden becomes the mother of all rivers and branches out to become the Pishon, Gihon, Tigris, and Euphrates— the waters that will feed and irrigate the empires and civilizations of the whole world. From Eden this river nurtures lands rich in gold, gum, resin, and cornelians and feeds the agriculture of all of Havilah, Cush, and Ashur. In Eden are found the headwaters supplying all of humanity with its bounty and its blossoms, for the garden in Eden and all the gardens of the world are only possible once God has sent water to irrigate the soil.

Eden's beauty is not limited to its flowers and trees. For God has also filled Eden with every sort of wild animal and every kind of bird imaginable and brought them before the human to be named. The pleasure park of Eden is not merely a garden but also a zoo and an aviary. Here is a place where humans can see lions, cheetahs, rhinos, hippos, giraffes, water buffalo, bison, tigers, zebras, monkeys, chimps, apes, baboons, and more kinds of deer, gazelle, elk, and moose than any traveler has ever spotted. Here is a garden with more fauna than any king has ever owned, any zoo has ever kept, or any safari has ever included. And in this garden one finds as well every kind of bird that has ever (or never) taken wing. Parrots, eagles, hawks, ospreys, owls, geese, ducks, woodpeckers, crows, hummingbirds, nightingales, peacocks, penguins, and thousands of others fill the branches and sky with their plumage and

---

[33] Jack Suggs, ed., *The Oxford Study Bible: Revised English Bible with the Apocrypha* (New York: Oxford University Press, 1992), footnote to Genesis 2:8, p. 12.

wings. Eden is a riot of color and forms, a rainbow of creatures, pressed down and overflowing with bounty and beauty.

And, finally, Eden is a place where the humans walk without shame or clothes. Their bodies are not hidden, and their nakedness is as natural—and as beautiful—as that of the cheetah or the swan. When Adam first spots Eve, he cries out in pleasure at the beauty of her flesh, and she is likewise drawn to him, no doubt finding him pleasing to the eye. Their bodies are beautiful, moving with the grace and ease of gazelles, reaching out to each other, tending to the garden, harvesting their food, and walking with the Lord God. For thousands of years, artists have admired and sought to capture the beauty of the human form— male and female, young and old, large and small—and in Eden this beauty shone forth unclothed and uncovered. The humans were part of the masterpiece of creation.

But the creation of Eden is also the creation of a peaceful and harmonious community—a just land—and this second creation narrative, like its predecessor, recounts the move from a violent and unjust society to one that is righteous and just. The creation account in Genesis 2:4b-25 begins with a barren world, where "there was neither shrub nor plant growing on the earth" and where "God had sent no rain; nor was there anyone to till the ground" (Gen 2:5)—not quite the chaos and desolation of *tohu wabohu*, but an infertile and inhospitable terrain nonetheless. Here was a place where no human would find sustenance or welcome, a land without promise or milk and honey.

Then God uses this same inhospitable soil to fashion the human (or earth creature) and places this living creature in a garden the Lord God has planted in Eden, a garden filled with every sort of vegetation for food. Now the human has a safe habitat, plenty of space to roam, an abundance of food to eat, an adequate supply of water for drinking and irrigation, and meaningful and productive work. These are significant strides on the path to a just community. The basic needs of humanity are being addressed, and the building blocks for human development have been supplied. The human has been granted life, food, drink, shelter, safety, and productive labor without toil or bondage.

But all is not right in Paradise. Seven times in the first creation account we read that "God saw that it was good" or "very good," but God's first comment about the creature in this creation story is "It is not good for the man to be *alone*" (Gen 2:18; emphasis added). The God who saw all of creation and each of its parts as beautiful in Genesis 1:1–2:4 does not find the aloneness of the human delightful. Instead, this aloneness is a disfigurement, like Richard III's hump. This aloneness is something ugly, something unnatural and frightening to behold. The living creature is somehow less than human because of this aloneness. The beauty of the humans in Genesis 1:27 is tied to their being made male and female, to their being fashioned as a couple, as a community or society; that is why one can claim that they are made in the image of God. They embody and reflect the Creator's beauty—they image God to the world—because they are a community. But this solitary creature, this lone human, is not beautiful, because it is not with others.

In Mary Shelley's classic tale of gothic horror, Victor Frankenstein is repulsed by the monstrous ugliness of the living creature he has fashioned, filling his heart "with breathless horror and disgust."

> No mortal could support the horror of that countenance. A mummy again endued with animation could not be so hideous as that wretch. I had gazed on him while unfinished; he was ugly then, but when those muscles and joints were rendered capable of motion, it became a thing such as even Dante could not have conceived.[34]

But the real disfigurement of Frankenstein's creature (whom Victor does not even have the courtesy to name) flows from the fact that he is alone. In Shelley's tale the creature has become a monster not because he has been fashioned by the hand of man, or because his parts are not well apportioned, but because he has been left alone—abandoned first by his maker and then by all of humanity. "Misery," the creature cries, "has made me a fiend."[35] And this misery is the result of his being everywhere excluded from human company. He is alone, miserably alone, spurned and abhorred.

Like Frankenstein's creation, the aloneness of the living creature points to a certain wildness, a violence that threatens to boil over and destroy. When the Lord God says that it is not good that the creature is alone, there is a recognition that the child who is abandoned, spurned, or left alone is likely to walk into a high school cafeteria or climb up a tower with a high-powered rifle. As the neighbors of such lonely teenagers inevitably report on the next day's evening news, "He was kind of a loner. Kept to himself a lot. Not many friends."

[34] Mary Shelley, *Frankenstein* (New York: Penguin Books, 1963), 56–57.
[35] Ibid., 95–96.

This aloneness is also reminiscent of Orson Welles's film *Citizen Kane*. For in this American cinema classic, Charles Foster Kane has everything *but* company. Alone and friendless, the newspaper magnate and millionaire dies atop the largest pile of toys and wealth ever assembled, an Eden furnished with all the great art and sculptures of the world, but without the solace of a single companion. Looking down at Kane's sprawling and cavernous Xanadu, God might well have repeated the line from Genesis 2:18: "It is not good for the man to be alone."

The human who is alone represents a violent and unjust society, a Hobbesian jungle where every hand is turned against the next, and life is "solitary, poor, nasty, brutish, and short."[36] This is the tyranny of anarchy, where there are no rights, no justice, and where every other person is a stranger or an enemy—where no one is a friend.

So it is that God decides to create a companion for the human, to fashion "a partner suited to him" (Gen 2:18). And when the menagerie of birds and animals falls short of the friendship the creature will need to be fully human, God transforms the solitary being into a couple, a society, a community. Now the creature is *not* alone, and the society of humans moves away from violence and injustice toward a just community.

This move is completed when the creature recognizes the humanity of the stranger placed before him. For when Adam says, "This one at last is bone from my bones, flesh from my flesh!" (Gen 2:23) he is acknowledging that this other (who is the rest of the human race) is his neighbor, his partner, his companion—and this recognition (which is mutual in this case) is what makes the creatures human.

For our greatest inhumanity, our most degrading ugliness and injustice, is always accompanied by our failure to recognize the humanity of the stranger, our failure to see the other (no matter how different his or her flesh) as neighbor, partner, or companion. This is the injustice of the Pharisee who fails to recognize he *is* like the tax collector, the injustice of the rich man who will not see the beggar Lazarus at his gate as his neighbor, and the injustice of the priest and Levite who do not notice that the wounded man on the roadside is their neighbor. Whenever humans prepare to abuse, oppress, or slaughter other humans, we first transform the objects of our violence or injustice into strangers, aliens, or enemies—and the best way to do this is to convince ourselves that

---

[36] Thomas Hobbes, *Leviathan* (Indianapolis, IN: Hackett Publishing Co., 1994), 76.

they are not "bone from my bones, [or] flesh from my flesh." This is the lesson of Darfur, Rwanda, Serbia, Northern Ireland, Dachau, Selma, and 9/11. We become monsters when we fail to see the stranger as neighbor, companion, and partner.

The story of the creation of Eden, then, is not merely the tale of a beautiful garden filled with lovely creatures. It is also the story of the creation of a just society, moving, first, from a barren and inhospitable wilderness to a lush garden that supports many (but not all) of humanity's needs and, second, from a violent and unjust collection of isolated strangers to a loving community of friends, partners, and neighbors who recognize and honor the humanity and dignity of others—and in doing so become fully human themselves. In Carlo Collodi's classic children's tale, Pinocchio becomes a real boy when he shows concern for others. In Genesis 2:4b-25 the living creatures fashioned from the soil become fully human when they recognize and respond to the humanity of others, making them in that moment a just society.

We can infer from Adam's proclamation and from what follows that the man and the woman were at peace with one another and thus in right relation to one another. It would have been no curse upon Eve to make her husband her master if that had been their original condition, so in Eden the humans must have been equal partners and companions, with neither lording it over nor oppressing the other. Likewise, it seems fair to assume that before the Fall both the husband and wife longed equally for each other, and that their love (and relationship) was mutual and supportive.

We can also infer from what happens in Genesis 3 that in Eden the humans are in harmony with God (who walks with them in the evening and before whom they are naked), with other creatures (whom they have named and who are their companions), and with the rest of creation (which they are to tend and which provides them with their daily bread without endless toil). The fact that the humans will only have to toil "all the days of your life" (Gen 3:14) after the Fall suggests that they—like all free people—are able to enjoy a Sabbath rest of contemplation and worship. Thus, Eden, far more than a beautiful garden, is a place where humans work and live in peaceful harmony with each other, with other creatures, and with their God. This is a masterpiece of justice. Indeed, as the creation of Sabbath in Genesis 1:1–2:4a introduces us to an age of beauty and justice, the creation of Eden in Genesis 2:4b-25 introduces us to a realm of beauty and justice.

"A Land Flowing with Milk and Honey": The Beauty of the Promised Land as a Righteous Community

The story of the deliverance of the Hebrews from their bondage in Egypt is also a tale of beauty and justice, for the Promised Land to which they will be delivered by God's liberating hand will—like Eden—be a place of beauty and justice, and indeed the beauty of this land will be the fruit of its justice.

In the final third of Frank Capra's *It's a Wonderful Life*, George Bailey (Jimmy Stewart) awakens to a nightmare in which his lovely hometown of Bedford Falls (a New England village straight out of a Norman Rockwell painting) has been transformed into something vulgar, cheap, and ugly—a gray and grimy Potterville (or potter's field—a cemetery) full of tenements, pool halls, bars, and brothels. In the place of a vibrant community where most folks (thanks to Bailey Savings and Loan) owned their own homes and had a small patch of green to garden and plenty of playgrounds and parks and ponds where their children could run and dance and swim, George Bailey discovers a seedy, worn-out landscape populated by impoverished, desperate, miserable souls—a field of nightmares.

The ugliness Capra tries to capture is the brutality of injustice, the disfigurement of a town eaten away by the greed of a few and the sufferings of the many. In Potterville the local banker has bought up every piece of property, forced the foreclosure of every other business, turned every homeowner into a tenant, and stolen the town's dreams and hopes. This is, in Capra's eyes, an ugly thing to see.

The authors of Genesis and Exodus offer a similar vision of the ugliness and injustice of Egypt, which the pharaohs and their retainers have transformed into a huge plantation where a sea of peasants and slaves toil on their master's lands and build their ruler's store cities, watching helplessly as food is taken out of their children's mouths, lashes are put to their backs, and the corpses of their infant sons float down the Nile. In Genesis 47 we read how Joseph and the pharaoh use a famine to extort money, livestock, and lands from the peoples of Egypt and Canaan, and how these same desperate farmers surrender their own freedom and future to keep their families alive, becoming sharecroppers and indentured servants on the pharaoh's vast tracts of stolen land. And in Exodus 1 we learn how subsequent pharaohs scapegoat and enslave the Hebrews, oppressing them with backbreaking labor and slaughtering their sons. In a few short chapters the land that had drawn Jacob and his sons becomes a vast, ugly wasteland of injustice where the children of farmers and shepherds have been reduced to an army of serfs and slaves. For as far as the eye can see, Pharaohville has become a nightmare of hunger, poverty, and oppression.

And God, who was not pleased to see the loneliness of Adam, is also not pleased by the ugliness of Pharaoh's Egypt. This time, though, the ugliness is experienced as sight and sound, the misery of the Hebrews and the discordant cry of a people under the lash. Like a mother awakened by a wailing child, the Lord God announces to Moses in Exodus 3 that she has been disturbed by the screams of her Hebrew children, beaten and abused by their Egyptian overseers. It is an ugly sound for God, one that does not please or delight her, and she will have Moses put an end to it. Beauty will be restored.

> The LORD said, "I have witnessed the misery of my people in Egypt and have heard them crying out because of their oppressors. I know what they are suffering and have come down to rescue them from the power of the Egyptians and to bring them up out of that country into a fine, broad land, a land flowing with milk and honey. . . . Now the Israelites' cry has reached me, and I have also seen how hard the Egyptians oppress them. Come, I shall send you to Pharaoh, and you are to bring my people Israel out of Egypt." (Exod 3:7-10)

So God promises to deliver the Hebrews from this ugly and unjust land and to bring them to a land of beauty and justice. Twenty times we read in Exodus, Leviticus, Deuteronomy, Numbers, Joshua, Jeremiah, and Ezekiel that God has searched out a land for the Hebrews, a good and spacious land, an exceedingly good land, a land flowing with milk and honey. And Ezekiel reports that this good and spacious place is (depending on the translation) the most beautiful of lands, the fairest of all lands, the loveliest of all lands, or a jewel among the lands. The Promised Land will be—particularly in the eyes of these liberated slaves and refugees—an exceedingly beautiful place. And when the Hebrews arrive at its edges and walk through its rich and rolling terrain, they—like God viewing creation—will see that it is exceedingly good (or delightful).

The land sought out by God and delivered to the Hebrews will be fertile and fruitful, rich and spacious, flowing with milk and honey, making it pleasing to the eye for these hungry refugees. But the real beauty of this good and spacious land is not merely topographical or even agricultural. Egypt produced rich harvests and fed an empire but withheld its abundance from those at the bottom. The beauty of the Promised Land will be the beauty of a free and just society where the goods of the earth are abundantly shared by *all* its residents and where the chaos and ugliness of slavery and war and poverty are replaced by the beauty of justice and peace and bounty. For the liberation of the Hebrews is not merely their deliverance from one land to another; it involves their transformation from a mob of impoverished, hoarding slaves into a society of free and fair people.

What makes the Promised Land beautiful is not simply that it is a well-watered land with rich soil, producing huge harvests and bumper crops. The beauty of the Promised Land, as the author of Deuteronomy 15:4-5 writes, is that in this place "there will never be any poor among you," that the scourges of poverty, debt, hunger, and slavery will be at an end, that in this land the tyranny, injustice, and inhospitality of Pharaoh will be a thing of the past.

For the Promised Land is much more than a piece of terrain. It is a society, a people—and this society will be as different as possible from the bondage in Egypt. The Promised Land will be a just community, a beautiful land where ex-slaves and refugees will find peace, justice, and security. And to build this new society, this masterpiece of beauty and justice, God will fashion something new and wonderful from the chaos and violence of Pharaoh's Egypt. Using this ragtag collection of Hebrews as clay, God will create a new community, a new land, where the beauty of justice will shine forth like a diadem.

In Genesis 1:1–2:4 the architect of creation fashions a beautiful three-tiered temple, separating water, sky, and air into separate realms and furnishing them with every sort of living creature, each sustained with ample food and habitat and all living together in an overarching harmony. In Exodus, Leviticus, and Deuteronomy the Lord God is the architect of a just society, instructing the Hebrews in the practices and rules they will need to enter and then sustain the Promised Land flowing with milk and honey. For the deliverance of the Hebrews is not just a matter of taking them out of Egypt; it is also a question of taking Egypt out of them, stripping them of the beliefs, practices, and laws of empire and teaching them the ways and practices of the Promised Land.

Fashioning the Promised Land

Exodus reports that the people who depart from Egypt are not the same people who arrive in Canaan. This is a new generation, one from which the sins and flaws of the previous generation have been purged. They are a people transformed, a people made ready to leave Egypt and the ways of empire behind, a people no longer afraid to enter the Promised Land. The time in the wilderness, the time spent on the brink of Canaan, has been used by the architect of the Promised Land to teach and transform the Hebrews, to fashion them into a people prepared to enter and become God's Promised Land, a society where milk and honey will flow in such abundance that widows and orphans and aliens will have enough to eat.

To effect this transformation, God will introduce several practices that will form the foundations of the Promised Land. Out in the wilderness God will teach these frightened refugees to stop hoarding food and to begin to share the earth's bounty, ensuring that every person and family has enough to eat. Away from their overseers and taskmasters, God will teach these former slaves to work together as free women and men, laboring as artisans and craftsmen who can rest when they are weary and bring a full range of talents and gifts to their work. Gathered around the ark of the covenant, God will introduce the Hebrews to a new form of worship, one that pays homage to God by practicing justice toward the poor and oppressed in their midst. Delivered from Pharaoh's plantations, God will instruct these former sharecroppers and tenant farmers how to institute land reform, distributing goodly portions of rich land to every tribe and family, keeping them free from poverty, hunger, and debt. And as they move into the Promised Land, God will teach them to reject the tyranny of kings and embrace a rule of law enforced by judges charged to treat all people fairly.

In Exodus 16:15-18 the Hebrews are provided with food by God to sustain them during their sojourn in the wilderness. But they are to collect and consume this food according to God's rules, which forbid hoarding. Moses instructs them to gather only what each person needs; and at the end of this daily gathering, every family—no matter how much they have collected—has just enough to provide each person with a sufficient ration. "Those who had gathered more had not too much, and those who had gathered less had not too little." In other words, the Hebrews are learning to share and not hoard their food. No longer terrified that Pharaoh and his overseers will take their food or that their fellow slaves will rob them, they are learning to share, to make sure that no one in their midst is hungry, that no one goes without.

Beginning in Exodus 25, the Hebrews are directed to build the ark of the covenant. This is not the first (or largest) public work these former slaves have been tasked to build. Pharaoh had them build his store cities and other great projects. But it is the first work they do as a free people, collecting the materials and funds needed by taking up a freewill offering, using one of their own people as chief engineer of the project, and adopting a Sabbath schedule that gives them a day of rest and worship never offered to slaves. In giving them this task, God is teaching the Hebrews to labor as artisans and free people.[37]

Out in the desert, the frightened Hebrews cling to the idolatrous worship of Egypt, fashioning a golden calf in imitation of their former masters. But Yahweh teaches them a new form of worship, one that honors the God who hears the cries of the poor and delivers slaves. This worship, Isaiah later reminds them, demands that they practice God's liberating and merciful justice by coming to the aid of the widow, orphan, and alien in their midst (Isa 58:6-7). Otherwise, their worship will be a sham despised and rejected by their God (Jer 7:4-7; Amos 5:21-4).

As the Hebrews prepare to move into Canaan, God has Joshua instruct them to apportion a fair share of the land to each family and tribe (Exod 25:13-18). After Pharaoh had extorted all the land of Egypt (Gen 47), the people were reduced to tenant farmers and sharecroppers on his vast plantations; but here every family and tribe will have their own parcel of land, and no one will be allowed to covet their neighbor's land (Deut 5:20) or move the boundary markers that fence off one landowner from another (Deut 19:14).

Finally, moving into the Promised Land, God has Moses appoint judges to govern the people and enforce their laws, rejecting the rule of kings or pharaohs. And these judges—unlike Pharaoh, who scapegoated the Hebrews, stripped them of their freedom, and murdered their children—are to treat Hebrew and alien alike, protecting the rights of the stranger as they do the rights of their own people. Here there will be no king but Yahweh, and one law and justice for all people (Deut 1:13-18).

Maintaining the Promised Land

In Genesis 1:27-28 God commissions humans as cocreators and stewards, instructing them to fashion other creatures in the divine image and maintain the order and harmony of creation. In Genesis 2:15 God charges humans with tending the beauty of creation, placing them in Eden to tend and care for this garden. So, too, after molding the clay of these

---

[37] Ellen F. Davis, "Slaves or Sabbath-Keepers? A Biblical Perspective on Human Work," *Anglican Theological Review* 83, no. 1 (January 1, 2001).

Hebrew slaves and refugees into a just and harmonious society, God commissions them as stewards, teaching them a set of practices with which they are to tend and maintain the beauty of this land.

First, they are to remember and show hospitality to the widow, orphan, and alien in their midst, providing sustenance, shelter, and security to the oppressed, marginalized, and needy. For, as Deuteronomy and Leviticus remind them on several occasions, they had once been such widows, orphans, and aliens, and the Lord their God rescued them from the inhospitality and cruelty of their overseers and delivered them to a land flowing with milk and honey.

Second, they are to establish a regular tithe for widows, orphans, and aliens. Deuteronomy 26:12 tells the Hebrews that every three years they are to set aside a tithe of their produce and give it over "to the Levites and to the aliens, the fatherless, and the widows so that they may eat in your settlements and be well fed."

Third, at harvest time the Hebrews are to leave the gleanings of their crops and vineyards for the poor and the alien. After going through their fields once, farmers are to let the poor and the alien reap and pick what is left over and what has fallen upon the ground (Lev 19:9-10). In this way those without land or work will be able to feed themselves, and those with enough will have shown they remember the Lord their God.

Fourth, since so many fell into bondage and slavery through debt, God instructs the Hebrews to be generous in their loans to the poor and to cancel these debts every seven years (Deut 15:7-12). Moreover, they are not to charge interest on loans to a poor neighbor or to keep the poor person's cloak as a security, lest he freeze (Exod 22:24-26). If they fail to keep these commands, the Promised Land will not be free of poverty, and God will hear the cries of these poor neighbors.

Fifth, unlike Pharaoh's slaves, who have no day of rest (Exod. 5:3-5) but toil all the days of their lives, God demands that the Hebrews extend a Sabbath rest to every member of the household, male and female, free and slave. In Deuteronomy 5:14 the Hebrews are instructed, "[On the Sabbath] you must not do any work, neither you, nor your son or your daughter, your slave or your slave-girl, your ox, your donkey, or any of your cattle, or the alien residing among you, so that your slaves and slave-girls may rest as you do."

Sixth, to repair the accumulated injuries of greed and injustice and to ensure that those who fall into poverty, debt, homelessness, and bondage are not permanently trapped in these conditions, God has the Hebrews institute Sabbatical and Jubilee years. Every seventh year, the Hebrews are to cancel the debts of their poor neighbors and free any Hebrews who have become their indentured servants, sending them on their way with a liberal supply "from your flock, from your threshing-floor and your winepress" (Deut 15:14). And every fiftieth year the Hebrews are also to restore the ancestral lands of those poor neighbors who have lost their property through debt and poverty, and to release any Hebrew slaves in their service (Lev 25:8-55).[38]

Seventh, going even further than the Sabbatical and Jubilee demands to release Hebrew debt slaves, God instructs the Hebrews in Leviticus 25:35-55 not to treat any debt-ridden Hebrew as a slave, but to take him or her on as a hired hand. And in Deuteronomy 23:15-16, God instructs the Hebrews to offer safe refuge to any escaped slave. "You must not surrender to his master a slave who has taken refuge with you. Let him stay with you anywhere he chooses in any one of your settlements, wherever suits him best; you must not force him."

And finally, to restrain the greed and injustice within people's hearts that forever threatens to undo the beauty and justice of the Promised Land, God forbids the coveting of other people's property and goods. Hebrews are not to covet their neighbors' fields (Deut 5:20), and the wealthy—for whom this is an endless temptation—are warned against coveting the lands and livestock of the poor and plotting on their couches to steal the fields and farms of their poor neighbors.[39] This covetous greed is a cancer on the beauty of the Promised Land and will transform it into something ugly and savage, where crops will not grow and harvests will fail.[40]

In the end, the Promised Land is a frail masterpiece, a living work of art that must be constantly watered and tended by compassion and justice if it is to sustain its beauty and keep from descending into the *tohu wabohu* of Pharaoh's empire. Again and again the prophets warn Israel of the danger of the destruction of this masterpiece if the people fail to keep the promise of its Creator and their liberator. The beauty of this good and spacious land, of what Ezekiel calls "the fairest of all lands" (Ezek 20:15), is to be found in the justice of its God and its people.

[38] Lowery, *Sabbath and Jubilee*, 57–77.

[39] Patrick D. Miller, "Property and Possession in Light of the Ten Commandments," in *Having: Property and Possession in Religious and Social Life*, ed. William Schweiker and Charles Mathewes (Grand Rapids, MI: Eerdmans, 2004), 45–46.

[40] See Isa 5:8; Mic 21:1-2; Amos 4; 5:11-17; 8:4-14.

A Heavenly Banquet:
The Beauty and Justice of the Reign of God

The Reign of God

In Exodus the Lord God promises to liberate the Hebrews from bondage and deliver them to a good and spacious land "flowing with milk and honey"—the fairest of all lands, as Ezekiel puts it—a land rich in justice and mercy, where there will be no poor and no tyrant king and where all will be provided for and none will be permanently trapped in servitude or homelessness. This land will be as different from Pharaoh's empire as day from night.

In the gospels Jesus comes announcing the reign or kingdom of God, a reign—like the Promised Land—that will liberate the world's lowly and oppressed from every sort of bondage and deliver them to a kingdom as different as possible from the empires of the world. And like the good and spacious land that God finds for the lowly and enslaved Hebrews, the reign of God will be good news for the world's poor, marginalized, and oppressed. It will be like a sumptuous banquet at which the world's hungry will receive a bounty of rich food and sweet wine, where the world's outcasts will find places of honor, and where the world's oppressed will be waited upon by their masters.

In Luke 4:18 Jesus announces to those gathered in the synagogue in Nazareth that he has come to preach "good news to the poor, to proclaim release for the prisoners and recovery of sight for the blind; to let the broken victims go free, to proclaim the year of the Lord's favour." This liberating "good news" Jesus brings to the world's poor, imprisoned, sick, and oppressed is the announcement of the reign of God, a kingdom that will be a Jubilee year in which not only are debts cancelled, lands returned, and slaves set free, but also the lame, blind, and sick are cured and aliens, refugees, and outcasts are offered hospitality.[41]

And just as the Hebrew refugees inherit the good and spacious land promised them by God, the world's poor are to inherit the kingdom of God. As Jesus notes in Luke 6:20, the kingdom of God belongs to the poor, and those who hunger and suffer and are cast out of society today will be welcomed into its warm embrace. For, as we read in James 2:5, the kingdom of God is promised to "those who are poor in the eyes of the world."

---

[41] See Matt 11:4-6; Luke 7:21-23.

To capture the radical beauty and justice of God's kingdom, Jesus turns again and again to the metaphor of a banquet table. Here the bounty of a rich and fertile land is brought to the table, where bowls and plates are filled with heaping portions of good food and where guests are welcomed and showered with lavish hospitality. The kingdom of God, Jesus reports in his parables, is like a sumptuous banquet at which unimaginable pleasures and honors will be provided to its guests. And these guests—unlike those at any other dinner table—will be the uncounted and unwashed masses who spend their lives fighting for scraps of spoiled food and going to bed hungry. At this banquet table the hungry, crippled, blind, lowly, and enslaved will find places of honor, be dressed and waited upon as royals, and be served a feast beyond their wildest imagination. As Paul writes in 1 Corinthians 2:9, "Scripture speaks of 'things beyond our seeing, things beyond our hearing, things beyond our imagining, all prepared by God for those who love him.'"

To the hungry, oppressed, and outcast souls who are to inherit the kingdom of God and receive places of honor at this table, the banquet Jesus describes must look as good and spacious as the Promised Land looks to the Hebrews coming out of their long sojourn in the desert, or as the bounty of creation and Eden seem to God after the desolate wasteland of *tohu wabohu.*

Indeed, the beauty of the kingdom of God is so striking, so arresting, that those who truly see it are captivated and entranced by it. They cannot turn away from it or pull back from its summons. As Keats describes Cortez and his men seeing the Pacific for the first time, the one who beholds the kingdom of God looks on "with a wild surmise," stunned into silence.[42] For the kingdom is like a treasure or pearl of great price—it is something marvelous and wondrous—and so anyone who turns away from this beauty, who makes up an excuse to back away, is not worthy of the kingdom (Luke 9:59-62).

But, like the beauty of the Promised Land, the beauty (and attraction) of God's kingdom cannot be seen by those who are unjust or unworthy. Just as the Hebrews had to undergo transformation before they could see this good and spacious land, so too Jesus tells the Pharisee Nicodemus, "No one can see the kingdom of God unless he has been born again" (John 3:3). Indeed, Jesus repeatedly affirms that the kingdom of God is

---

[42] John Keats, "On First Looking into Chapman's Homer," in Quiller-Couch, Arthur Thomas, Sir. *The Oxford Book of English Verse* (Oxford: Clarendon, 1919, [1901]); Bartleby.com, 1999. www.bartleby.com/101/. [October 2, 2007].

a hidden beauty, invisible to those who see and judge as the world sees and judges. It is a small beauty, as tiny as a mustard seed (Luke 13:18-19). It is a secret beauty, hidden in cryptic parables and unseen by those who look for signs (Mark 4:11; Luke 8:9-11; 17:20-35). To see the beauty of the kingdom of God, our hearts and eyes must be changed and opened.

The beauty of great art is sometimes difficult for us to see because it demands something from us. The art of popular culture often provides beauty that is easy to access, requiring little effort to engage or understand. Such art entertains us without expecting anything from us. But to really appreciate and be transformed by the beauty of great art, we often need to make some effort, to step beyond the settled patterns of our lives, to open ourselves up to risk, suffering, loss, and the depth of human experience.

The beauty of the kingdom of God makes such demands upon us, calling for us to be born again, to pick up our cross and follow after Jesus, to see our neighbor in the face of the foreigner, stranger, and enemy. It is a stark beauty, or to paraphrase Dostoevsky, "a harsh and dreadful" beauty.[43] It is a topsy-turvy beauty in which all those at the bottom of the world's pyramids will be gathered into the bosom of Abraham, but all those clinging to power, wealth, and advantage and ignoring the cries of their sisters and brothers will find themselves unceremoniously tossed out into the darkness, where there will be wailing and gnashing of teeth.

To savor the beauty of the kingdom of God, one must be stripped of all acquisitiveness, purged of arrogance and power, cleansed of any attachments to the present order and to the advantages of class, race, and gender. One must, as Jesus says, become like a child, a powerless and humble creature without titles or wealth: "Truly I tell you: unless you turn round and become like children, you will never enter the kingdom of Heaven. Whoever humbles himself and becomes like this child will be the greatest in the kingdom of Heaven, and whoever receives one such child in my name receives me" (Matt 18:3-5).

Not surprisingly, there are many who cannot or will not see this beauty, who cannot and will not enter the kingdom of God. Those who are rich and powerful, who have accumulated great wealth, and who have insulated themselves from the cries of the poor will not be able to enter the kingdom of God.[44] The self-righteous, who do not recognize that

---

[43] Fyodor Dostoevsky, *The Karamazov Brothers* (London: Wordsworth Editions, 2007), 59.

[44] See Matt 19:23-24; Mark 10:23-25; Luke 16:19-31; 18:25-25.

sinners and outcasts are their neighbors, are stunned to discover that such lowlifes are entering the kingdom of God ahead of them and may even be taking their places (see Matt 21:32). And the indifferent, who have never recognized the broken and injured bodies of their neighbors as "bone from my bones and flesh from my flesh" are turned away from the kingdom (see Matt 25:31-46).

The beauty that makes such stark demands upon us is the radical justice of the kingdom of God. Just as the Hebrews could not enter the Promised Land until they were transformed into a just people, so the beauty of the kingdom of God makes demands upon those who would see it and enter it—that they become just. "For the kingdom of God is not eating and drinking, but justice, peace, and joy, inspired by the Holy Spirit" (Rom 14:17).

And so we read in 1 Corinthians 6:9-10, Galatians 5:21, and Ephesians 5:5 that the wicked cannot enter the kingdom of God. According to these passages, the kingdom of God belongs to the poor and welcomes the loving, peaceful, patient, kind, and good; but swindlers, thieves, and the greedy find no place there.

Just as God helps the Hebrews to appreciate and protect the beauty and justice of the Promised Land by teaching them a set of practices, so too Jesus instructs his disciples in the ways of practicing and protecting the beauty of the kingdom of God. The practices Jesus passes on to his disciples, however, center not around the cultivation of the land and its produce but around the tables to which this produce comes and at which the people gather to share and eat this food. Jesus will teach his disciples a set of table manners, helping them to transform themselves into hosts, guests, and servants fit for the banquet of the kingdom of God.

In his parables about the reign of God and in his own behavior at table, Jesus offers his disciples three sets of table manners: (1) hospitality to needy strangers, (2) friendship to outcasts, and (3) service to the lowly.

HOSPITALITY TO THOSE IN NEED: MAKING ROOM FOR THE POOR

The first of Jesus' table manners is hospitality to those in need. In the infancy narratives of Matthew and Luke, Jesus is someone who knows about the harms of inhospitality, for he was born in a stable and driven into exile by a murderous tyrant.[45] So it is perhaps not surprising that

---

[45] See Matt 2:13-18; Luke 2:1-7.

the one "with no place to lay his head" should direct his disciples to offer hospitality to any needy strangers they encounter.

In the six accounts of the feeding miracles that occur in the gospels, a large crowd has followed Jesus and the Twelve out to a remote place, and as evening draws on, the disciples grow anxious about providing food for such a great number of strangers and advise Jesus to dismiss his audience.[46] But Jesus instructs the Twelve to "find something to feed them yourselves," and he later directs them to seat, serve, and pick up after the thousands who have been fed. In this way Jesus teaches his frightened disciples to provide hospitality to those in need, imitating the hospitality of God, who "shows love towards the alien . . ., giving him food and clothing" (Deut 10:18) and of Sarah and Abraham, who "entertained angels" in Genesis 18.

When invited to dinner at the house of a local Pharisee, Jesus instructs his host to offer a radical hospitality that does not imitate the self-ingratiating practice of the day but welcomes those in desperate need. "When you are having guests for lunch or supper, do not invite your friends, your brothers or other relations, or your rich neighbours; they will only ask you back again and so you will be repaid. But when you give a party, ask the poor, the crippled, the lame, and the blind. That is the way to find happiness, because they have no means of repaying you. You will be repaid on the day when the righteous rise from the dead" (Luke 14:12-13).

And when a legal expert inquires of Jesus how he might gain eternal life (or enter the kingdom of God), Jesus recounts the parable of the Good Samaritan—a man who shows extraordinary hospitality to a wounded stranger by the roadside, providing him with care, comfort, and lodging beyond anything that might be expected of him—and directs the lawyer to go and do likewise (Luke 10:25-37).

The notion that hospitality is an essential practice for anyone interested in entering the kingdom of God is driven home by Matthew's parable of the sheep and the goats. Here the Son of Man invites those who have provided food to the hungry, clothing to the naked, shelter to the homeless, and comfort to the sick and the imprisoned to enter the kingdom of God, while turning away those who fail to do so (Matt 25:31-46).

The early church understands that Jesus directs them to take up the radical hospitality of the kingdom of God and to take care of those in need. In Luke 24 the two disciples on the road to Emmaus recognize the

[46] Matt 14:13-18; 15:29-39; Mark 6:30-44; 8:1-10; Luke 9:10-17; John 6:1-14.

risen Christ in the breaking and sharing of the bread, remembering, no doubt, the Lord who instructs them to share their food with the hungry multitudes. And in chapters 2 and 4 of Acts we read that the church in Jerusalem gathers for the "breaking of the bread" and practices such a radical hospitality that there is no one in need in their midst. Hospitality to the needy stranger is essential for anyone seeking the kingdom of God.

FRIENDSHIP: WELCOMING THE OUTCASTS AND SINNERS

The second set of table manners Jesus teaches his disciples has to do with showing friendship to outcasts. Time and time again we read in the gospels that Jesus and his disciples break bread with public sinners of every stripe; the inclusive nature of what some have called his "radical table fellowship" was a source of scandal and offense to many.

We tend to invite our friends and colleagues to break bread with us, and we tend to associate with folks of like mind, taste, and class. This tendency produces a sort of table hierarchy that excludes those who are "not like us" or who fail to meet our standards. Jesus lived in a world where many practiced a "politics of purity"[47] that kept the sinful and unclean away from their tables, and he violated that practice over and over again, having dinner at the houses of tax collectors like Levi and Zacchaeus and allowing a public sinner to come and wash his feet while dining at the house of Simon the Pharisee.[48]

For Jesus, the kingdom of God is not satisfied with the friendship we extend only to our neighbors and coreligionists. Instead, Jesus demands a friendship of his disciples that is universal, catholic, radical, and boundless; it is a friendship that embraces prostitutes, tax collectors, and sinners and offers them places of honor at our tables. It is a friendship that offers love to our enemies and forgiveness to those who persecute us. It is a scandalous, terrifying friendship that does not insulate or protect us from the larger world outside our neighborhoods and gated communities, but tosses us out into public places and commands us to make friends with those who are not like us—and who do not like us.

When Jesus tells his disciples "I have called you friends" (John 15:15), he summons them to a radical friendship that is different from the friend-

---

[47] See Marcus J. Borg, *Meeting Jesus Again for the First Time* (San Francisco: HarperSanFrancisco, 1994), 49–61.

[48] Luke 5:27-39; 7:36-50; 19:1-10.

ship tied to blood, family, tribe, or nation. He summons them to a friendship that will lead the early church to welcome Samaritans, Greeks,
Romans, Africans, and peoples from the whole world into their midst.
And if they are to be members of what Paul calls the Body of Christ,
these Christians must overcome the divisions of race, class, and gender
so that in Christ—and in the kingdom of God—there will be neither Jew
nor Greek, neither slave nor free, neither male nor female; all will be one
in Christ.[49]

SERVICE TO THE LOWLY:
HUMILITY AND OVERCOMING HIERARCHIES

The final practice to be learned by those seeking to enter the kingdom
of God is service to the lowly, and this would seem to be the toughest of
the table manners the disciples of Jesus must master.

In the ancient world guests often fight over places of honor at
banquets,[50] and Jesus' disciples seem equally obsessed with securing the
best seats and highest rank possible. In Mark 9:33-37 they have been
squabbling about which of them is the greatest, and Jesus directs them
to reject the hierarchy of the world, replacing it with the lower-archy of
the kingdom of God.[51] "If anyone wants to be first," he tells them, "he
must make himself last of all and servant of all." The greatest person at
God's table will become a servant. This is a complete reversal of the disciples' expectations and of the world's table manners.

Jesus offers a similar lesson to the guests dining at the house of Simon
the Pharisee. "When you receive an invitation, go and sit down in the
lowest place, so that when your host comes he will say, 'Come up higher,
my friend.' Then all your fellow-guests will see the respect in which you
are held. For everyone who exalts himself will be humbled; and whoever
humbles himself will be exalted" (Luke 14:10-11). As we saw earlier,
those preparing to enter the kingdom of God must make themselves as
lowly and small as children.

And, as already noted, the six narratives of the feeding miracles have
Jesus training the disciples to become table servants, for in these various
accounts the Twelve are directed to seat, wait upon, and pick up after

---

[49] See Gal 3:28; Col 3:11.

[50] Dennis Smith, "Table Fellowship as a Literary Motif in the Gospel of Luke," *The
Journal of Biblical Literature* 106, no. 4 (1987): 617–20.

[51] See also Luke 9:46-48; Matt 18:1-5; 20:20-28; 23:6-12.

the large crowds that have followed Jesus into the wilderness. Still, the lesson is a hard one for the disciples, who at the Last Supper, according to Luke, are still arguing about who is the most important. Jesus responds to this squabbling by telling them that

> Among the Gentiles, kings lord it over their subjects; and those in authority are given the title Benefactor. Not so with you: on the contrary, the greatest among you must bear himself like the youngest, the one who rules like one who serves. For who is greater—the one who sits at table or the servant who waits on him? Surely the one who sits at table. Yet I am among you like a servant. (Luke 22:25-27)

Still, Jesus' most powerful instruction regarding this particular table manner comes in John 13:1-17, when he gets up from the table and begins to wash the disciples' feet, provoking an uproar from Peter, who is told that unless he learns this lesson of service, he will have nothing to do with Jesus—or, presumably, with the kingdom of God. After washing everyone's feet, Jesus then returns to his seat and tells the Twelve, "I have set you an example: you are to do as I have done for you" (John 13:15), setting a standard for them to follow in their treatment of others.

That the early church understood that this sort of service is required of those preparing for the kingdom of God is made clear in Acts 6, where we read that it is the role of the Twelve, who had been trained by Jesus to wait on table, to wait on the widows and orphans in the local church. Service of the lowly is a kingdom virtue.

Conclusion:
Four Biblical Visions of the Beauty of Justice

In the two Creation accounts, the story of the Promised Land, and the proclamation of the reign of God, the Bible offers four visions of the beauty of the righteous or just society. In each of these visions God fashions the masterpiece of a just society and invites us to become cocreators in the ongoing work of building and sustaining such a community.

That creation and Eden are works of beauty seems self-evident; but they are also works of justice—and indeed it can be argued that it is the justice of these communities that renders them so beautiful, that makes them so pleasing to the divine eye. For both creation and Eden move from chaos and desolation to cosmos and community, fashioning a world where not only the sky, sea, and land are held in harmonious balance but all the creatures live and work and play together, sharing food and habitat and companionship with one another.

That the Promised Land and the reign of God are realms of justice should also be self-evident, for those desiring to enter these kingdoms must undergo a transformation and take up the practice of justice, mercy, and peace. Still, Canaan is also a good and spacious land, a jewel among all other nations; and the kingdom of God is like a wedding feast full of extravagant foods and lavish costumes. They are both, in their own way, masterpieces of beauty—and their beauty is the justice and mercy of God brimming over and flowing down like pressed oil or rich honey.

These biblical visions offer up the justice and mercy of God as something wonderful, transformative, liberating, and enchanting, as something that draws us out of ourselves and our selfishness and pulls us into a righteous community.

Indeed, these visions suggest, in no small way, that the righteous community is the most powerful and basic sacrament of God—that when we see the beauty of the dance of the righteous, living and working and playing in peaceful and harmonious relations with one another, we are seeing the face of God.

Christians believe that we see the beauty of God in creation and that we see the face of Christ in the poor, the suffering, the stranger, and, indeed, the enemy. It also seems true that these four biblical visions of the beautiful and righteous community point to an underlying truth about the God in whose image and likeness we are fashioned: the righteous community is the sacrament that best captures the beauty of God, and wherever two or three of us are gathered together in peace and justice, there is the beauty of the face of God.

Chapter 2

A Right to Beauty:
Milk and Honey for the Souls of the Poor

The great crime which the moneyed classes and promoters of industry com-
mitted . . . was the condemning of workers to ugliness, ugliness, ugliness:
meanness and formless and ugly surroundings, ugly ideals, ugly religion,
ugly hope, ugly love, ugly furniture, ugly houses, ugly relationship between
workers and employers. The human soul needs actual beauty even more
than bread.
                    —D. H. Lawrence, "Nottingham and the Mining Country"

A Right to Beauty?

"The weakest of humanity," Gustavo Gutierrez once argued, must not
become "the rubbish tip of the industrialized nations," forced to live in
the squalor and filth manufactured and discarded by the world's elite.
For, the eminent liberation theologian noted, "the right to beauty is an
expression (more pressing than some suppose) of the right to life."[1]
Several years later the Vatican's Pontifical Council for Culture demanded
that the church engage "in the promotion of justice and building up the

---

[1] Gustavo Gutierrez, "The Task and Content of Liberation Theology," in *The Cam-*
bridge Companion to Liberation Theology (New York: Cambridge University Press), 36.

great common house where every creature is called to live, especially the poor: [for] they too have a right to beauty."[2]

A right to beauty? How curious that a leading liberation theologian and a Vatican document should both agree that the poor have a right to beauty when this claim appears almost nowhere else. Gutierrez and the Pontifical Council for Culture suggest that humans have a fundamental right to beauty and that the poor in particular must not be deprived of some access to the beauty of God's creation. And yet the United Nations' Universal Declaration of Human Rights makes no mention of a right to beauty, nor does Pope John XXIII's social encyclical *Peace on Earth*, considered by many to be the most comprehensive Catholic statement on human rights. Indeed, the word "beauty" does not appear in either document or in any other major document listing basic human rights.[3]

And yet Gutierrez and the Vatican are not alone in contending that human beings need some beauty in their lives and that the poor, so often drowning in a sea of filth and refuse, have a desperate need for some small ray of beauty. Philosophers and theologians have long argued that beauty engages and enlarges the human spirit, lifting us above and beyond the drudgery of our daily routines and opening us, if only momentarily, to the transcendent, the immortal, the divine. In this sense beauty elevates us above mere beasts of burden and helps render us more fully human. In her work *On Beauty and Being Just*, Elaine Scarry argues that beauty is sacred, surprising, and lifesaving, opening us up to the eternal; the twentieth-century theologian P. T. Forsyth contends that a religion stripped of beauty produces "a drought in our own souls."[4]

At the same time, advocates for social justice have consistently complained that the world's poor and oppressed are not only deprived of

[2] Pontifical Council for Culture, The *Via Pulchritudinis*, Privileged Pathway for Evangelisation and Dialogue, March 28, 2006, III.3.

[3] There is no reference to beauty in the International Covenant on Economic, Social and Cultural Rights, the International Covenant on Civil and Political Rights, the Bill of Rights of the United States Constitution, or the Declaration of the Rights of Man and Citizen of the French Revolution. Still, articles 24 and 27 of the Universal Declaration of Human Rights do defend the right of all to leisure, to freely participate in the cultural life of the community, and to enjoy the arts. As we will see below, these rights may suggest a right to beauty.

[4] Elaine Scarry, *On Beauty and Being Just* (Princeton, NJ: Princeton University Press, 2001), 23; P. T. Forsyth, *Religion in Recent Art* (London: Hodder and Stoughton, 1905), 7.

adequate food, clothing, shelter, and employment but constantly forced to live and work in degrading and demeaning ugliness. In the middle of the nineteenth century, Friedrich Engels railed against the living conditions of England's poor.

> The houses are occupied from cellar to garret, filthy within and without, and their appearance is such that no human being could possibly wish to live in them. But all this is nothing in comparison with the dwellings in the narrow courts and alleys between the streets . . . in which the filth and tottering ruin surpass all description. Scarcely a whole window pane can be found, the walls are crumbling, door posts and window frames loose and broken, doors of old boards nailed together, or altogether wanting. . . . Heaps of garbage and ash lie in all directions, and the foul liquids emptied before the doors gather in stinking pools. Here live the poorest of the poor.[5]

And this brutal ugliness was certainly not unique to England or the early stages of the Industrial Revolution; it can still be found in the teeming archipelagos of ghettos, barrios, slums, favelas, shanty towns, settlements, and refugee camps spread throughout the developing and developed world. At the end of the twentieth century, the philosopher Nicholas Wolterstorff echoed Engels's complaint, arguing that "the tragedy of modern urban life is not only that so many in our cities are oppressed and powerless, but also that so many have nothing surrounding them in which any human being could possibly take sensory delight."[6] And Pope John Paul II noted that the privileged of the world "continue to accumulate excess goods, squandering available resources, while masses of people are living in conditions of misery at the very lowest level of subsistence."[7]

Hunger, poverty, greed, oppression, disease, pollution, and violence create a world that is not only brutally unjust but horribly ugly, and this ugliness disfigures our planet and swamps the lives of millions and millions of poor forced to live and work in overcrowded, exhausted, and toxic squalor. This means, as the Brazilian theologian and pastor Abival

[5] Friedrich Engels, *The Condition of the Working Class in England in 1844* (London: George Allen & Unwin, Ltd., 1950), 27.

[6] Nicholas Wolterstorff, *Art in Action* (Grand Rapids, MI: Eerdmans, 1980), 82.

[7] John Paul II, Peace with God the Creator, Peace with All of Creation, January 1, 1990, no. 8.

Pires da Silveira has noted, that the crisis facing our world is not merely a crisis of justice but also a crisis of beauty.[8] And it means, as Gutierrez and the Vatican have argued, that the world's poor and oppressed have a claim not merely to justice but also to beauty.

The goal of this chapter is to show that all humans have a fundamental right to live and work in some modicum of beauty and that the poor have a special claim to a fair share of the world's beauty. To do this we will first look at the understanding of human rights found in Catholic Social Teaching, seeing if we can discover any basis for a right to beauty. Then we will offer three specific reasons for a universal and fundamental right to beauty: (1) the contemplative and self-transcending rest associated with beauty is essential to achieving our full humanity as persons; (2) the ability to create beauty is a fundamental human talent and need, without which we cannot fulfill our potential or vocation; and (3) persons and communities systematically deprived of beauty and the ability to create beauty have invariably been stripped of justice, as the pervasive presence of injustice produces an ugliness that disfigures persons and communities. Finally, we will argue that the world's poor have a particular need for beauty both because they suffer an unjust burden of ugliness in their lives and because their labor and creativity have produced so much of the world's beauty.

A Catholic Understanding of Human Rights

Aside from the 2006 statement by the Pontifical Council for Culture, Catholic Social Teaching does not mention or defend a specific right to beauty. Still, it may be possible to discover some grounds for a basic right to beauty within Catholic social thought. At the very least, it should be possible to find in these documents ample support for an argument that human beings should not be forced to live and work in conditions stripped of any semblance of beauty.

Catholic Social Teaching begins by arguing that human rights are universal and intrinsic. Like the Universal Declaration of Human Rights, Catholic social thought affirms that *every* human being has fundamental rights that flow from their nature as persons.[9] These rights are not

---

[8] Abival Pires da Silveira, "Justice, Bread and Beauty," *Reformed World* 47, nos. 3–4 (1997): 103.

[9] John XXIII, *Pacem in Terris*, no. 9.

dependent on citizenship, race, religion, gender, class, or age, but belong to everyone everywhere. These rights flow from our nature as free and intelligent beings *and* from the fact that we are fashioned in the image and likeness of God. No nation or community of nations, no church or corporation has given us these rights—and none can take them away. They belong to us as persons and cannot be denied without violating us and the communities to which we belong.

Catholic Social Teaching also subscribes to a comprehensive view of human rights, asserting that persons and communities are entitled both to the social and economic goods and services (like food, clothing, shelter, education, and medical care) required for us to survive and flourish as human beings and to the political and civil liberties (like freedom of speech, assembly, and religion) needed to fully participate in and contribute to a free society. Underlying this comprehensive vision of human rights is a holistic view of human persons as *embodied, social,* and *spiritual* beings who require both (1) a decent and reasonably comfortable environment where they can live and work with dignity and (2) the opportunity to develop their full range of talents and join with others in the creation of a just society.

Within this comprehensive view of human rights, two points suggest that persons may have a right to something like beauty—or at least a right not to be permanently entrapped in demeaning squalor.

First, Catholic documents do not merely assert that people have the right to enough food, clothing, shelter, education, health care and income to *survive*. Instead, time and time again the documents affirm that people have a right to "the means which are suitable to the *proper* development of [human] life"[10] and argue that the poor and the working class have a right to "decent" and "reasonably comfortable" accommodations and to living and working conditions that provide for their "dignity."[11] Elsewhere, the church has also expressed its opposition to "subhuman living conditions . . . [and] degrading working conditions," as they are "offenses against human dignity."[12] Indeed, church documents affirm the

[10] John XXIII, *Pacem in Terris*, no. 11, in David O'Brien and Thomas Shannon, *Catholic Social Thought: The Documentary History* (Maryknoll, NY: Orbis, 1997), 132; emphasis added.

[11] Leo XIII, *Rerum Novarum*, nos. 44–47.

[12] Second Vatican Council, *Gaudium et Spes, in Vatican Council II: The Basic Sixteen Documents*, ed. Austin Flannery, OP (Northport, NY: Costello Publishing Co., 1996), no. 27.

rights of all persons to living and working conditions that are safe, clean, and reasonably comfortable, and Pope John Paul II has asserted the right of all persons to a clean environment.[13] This would suggest that humans, unlike mere beasts of burden, are entitled to certain intangibles commensurate with their dignity as persons. And if such dignity does not require the presence of beauty in one's environment, it must at least reject an unrelenting ugliness.

Second, Catholic Social Teaching affirms the twin rights of development and participation,[14] affirming that all persons and communities have the right to fully develop their human talents and resources in ways that enable them to participate in and contribute to the larger political, economic, cultural, and religious structures of society.[15] In particular, church documents assert a right to cultural, artistic, and educational development allowing persons and communities to participate in and contribute to the common good. And beyond that, John Paul II argues that persons have a right to develop their "openness to the transcendent."[16]

As creatures fashioned in the image and likeness of the Creator of a world of beauty, humans require much more than mere sustenance and security. To become fully human we must be allowed to realize our gifts and talents, to fulfill our vocation as cocreators of beauty by working upon ourselves and by joining with others in the work of creating a just society—a labor that could, without exaggeration, be described as humanity's most important work of art. And so the right to development and participation certainly imply a right to become cocreators of beauty, while a right to develop into creatures open to the transcendent would seem to imply a right to some small beauty in our souls.

At the same time, Catholic social thought on human rights is shaped by the twin beliefs that every human being and community is entitled to a fair share of the goods of creation and that the poor and underprivileged need and deserve special assistance in securing their fair share.

Both the principle of the universal purpose of created goods and the principle of distributive justice demand that *all* persons and communities receive a fair share of the earth's goods—securing at least enough to

---

[13] John Paul II, *Laborem Exercens*, nos. 11, 21, and especially 19; John Paul II, Peace with God the Creator, Peace with All Creation, no. 9.

[14] John Paul II, *Sollicitudo Rei Socialis*, no. 32.

[15] John XXIII, *Pacem in Terris*, nos. 12–13.

[16] John Paul II, *Sollicitudo Rei Socialis*, no. 32, citing *Gaudium et Spes*, no. 69.

sustain and support them in reasonable comfort. As Paul VI writes in *Populorum Progressio,*

> Now if the earth truly was created to provide man with the necessities of life and the tools for his own progress, it follows that every man has the right to glean what he needs from the earth. The recent Council reiterated this truth: "God intended the earth and everything in it for the use of all human beings and peoples. Thus, under the leadership of justice and in the company of charity, created goods should flow fairly to all."[17]

And if, as we have already seen, God's creation is a world of beauty, it seems clear that all persons have a right not merely to the food and shelter provided from nature's warehouse, but also to some share of the beauty of God's bounty.

Catholic social thought has long asserted that the state has a special duty to protect the rights of the poor and oppressed, as they are too often unable to adequately provide for their own rights. And for over three decades, church documents have called upon all Christians to make a *preferential option for the poor* by standing in solidarity with them and taking up their cause in struggles for justice. Given, as we will see below, the systematic alienation of the world's poor from both enjoyment and creation of beauty, it seems reasonable to argue that any real preferential option for the poor would help them to secure not only liberation from poverty and oppression but also some minimal access to their fair share of beauty.

And so, while Catholic Social Teaching does not specifically address a right to beauty, there are a number of elements in the tradition that would suggest that all persons have a right to some fair share of the beauty of creation and to participation in the ongoing work of creating a world of beauty, and that the redemptive work of preaching the Good News must certainly involve making a preferential option for those standing outside beauty's gates.

If Catholic Social Teaching leads us to the brink of a basic right to beauty, three arguments may take us over the brink, making a clear case for this right. First, beauty provides a contemplative and self-transcending rest essential to achieving our full potential as humans. Becoming fully human involves opening ourselves to the transcendent and allow-

---

[17] Paul VI, *Populorum Progressio,* no. 22.

ing ourselves to be concerned with more than our own individual good, and beauty can call us beyond ourselves in both these ways. Second, the ability to create beauty and to join with others in helping to create a world of beauty is a fundamental human talent and need. Humans who are deprived of this ability are stripped of their vocation to be cocreators of beauty and reduced to a form of slavery. Third, everyone has a basic right to a fair share of the world of beauty created by God, and persons and communities systematically deprived of beauty and the ability to create beauty have invariably been stripped of justice, as the pervasive presence of injustice produces an ugliness that disfigures persons and communities.

The Right to a Contemplative and Self-Transcending Rest (Sabbath)

Beauty Draws Us out of the Mundane and Opens Us to the Transcendent

In *Six Great Ideas* Mortimer Adler argues that that the enjoyment of beauty provides us with the sort of contemplative and self-transcending rest humans need. "The contemplation of anything from which we derive the disinterested or spiritual pleasure of enjoyable beauty also introduces rest into our lives," and "the goodness of enjoyable beauty that makes it an indispensable ingredient in the happiness of a well-lived life consists in its providing us with the rest that all of us need."[18] According to Adler, sleep and relaxation allow our bodies and minds to recuperate from work and stress, but the enjoyment of beauty takes us out of our daily routines and may even "be said to lift us out of ourselves, resulting in a kind of ecstasy."[19] Turning to the theologians, Adler suggests that humans have a fundamental need for a rest that previews "the heavenly rest of the souls who enjoy in heaven the beatific vision of God"[20] and that the enjoyment of beauty provides just such a rest.

The nineteenth-century designer and social reformer William Morris wrote a great deal about people's need for and right to beauty, and we will see below how Morris argued for the right of all workers to labor that was fitting and honorable, meaning in part labor that produced

[18] Mortimer J. Adler, *Six Great Ideas* (New York: Touchstone, 1997 [1981]), 130.
[19] Ibid., 129.
[20] Ibid., 130.

works of beauty as well as utility. But Morris also contended that all people need not simply rest from their labors, but leisure, which would provide working men and women "with time for serious thought, for imagination—for dreaming even."[21] In addition, Morris argued that the working class requires beautiful and natural places where people might enjoy or create romance, poetry, and art, and he contended that without such leisure and wild places "the race of men will inevitably worsen."[22] Like Adler, Morris believes that humans need some contemplative rest or artful dreaming in which they might savor or create beauty, otherwise they will decline into something worse.

Elaine Scarry also believes that beauty takes us out of ourselves. As she sees it, the encounter with beauty knocks us out of our routines and inspires us both to wonder from whence this beauty comes and to become its herald by making endless copies of beauty everywhere we go.[23] Our encounter with a beauty that is sacred and unprecedented awakens awe in us and sets us off on a quest for beauty's source, an endless pilgrimage that led Plato, Aquinas, and Dante to associate beauty with the immortal and the divine. Scarry calls this process "deliberation," and though it differs from Adler's contemplation, it also draws us to the divine and transcendent. At the same time, beauty turns us into its disciples, calling us to take up the labor of creating more and more beauty, setting off an endless (and eternal?) series of creativity. Beethoven hears Mozart and is driven to compose symphonies. Michelangelo sees the Pantheon and must build St. Peter's. Beauty overflows and shines out, stunning us and sending us reeling in search of its source and in imitation of its grandeur. Beauty begets beauty, which begets beauty, which begets beauty; and having stumbled upon a link in this chain, we find ourselves climbing the ladder of beauty in search of the transcendent and building more and more rings till there is beauty everywhere.

In *Beauty: The Invisible Embrace*, John O'Donahue turns to etymology to show how beauty draws us out of ourselves. "In Greek," O'Donahue notes, "the word for the beautiful is *to kalon*. It is related to the word *kalein*, which includes the notion of 'call.' When we experience beauty we feel called. The Beautiful stirs passion and urgency in us, and calls

---

[21] William Morris, "Art, Socialism and Environment," in *The Green Studies Reader: From Romanticism to Ecocriticism*, ed. Lawrence Coupe (London: Routledge, 2000), 35.

[22] Ibid., 35.

[23] Scarry, *On Beauty and Being Just*, 28–30.

us forth from aloneness into the warmth and wonder of an eternal embrace."[24]

Beauty "Unselfs" Us

But Scarry goes further than Adler, claiming that beauty does not merely open us up to the transcendent or provide us with a contemplative (and "deliberative") rest, but pulls us outside of ourselves, drawing us toward a more selfless and egalitarian view of the world and the neighbor. Relying on language borrowed from Iris Murdoch, Scarry argues that beauty "unselfs" us, dislodging us from the center of our own universe and opening us up to concern for the other. According to Murdoch, beauty is one of "the most obvious things in our surroundings which is an occasion for 'unselfing.' "[25] Caught in the sudden grip of beauty, we are momentarily unconcerned with ourselves or with defending our ego. Cast to the side by beauty's radiance, we are no longer the heroic protagonist of our own story but a minor character standing with the rest of humanity's throng. Beauty dethrones us and renders us one of the crowd. Even more amazingly, Scarry notes, we accept beauty's unselfing somewhat joyfully, experiencing it not so much as an unwanted demotion, but as something sweet and pleasant. Indeed, beauty may be unique in its ability to displace and please us simultaneously, preparing us, Scarry thinks, for the pleasures of justice.

Scarry finds Murdoch's notion of beauty's unselfing power echoed in the work of Simone Weil, who speaks of beauty's capacity to "decenter" us. Beauty, Weil reports, demands that we "give up our imaginary position as the center. . . . A transformation then takes place at the very roots of our sensibility, in our immediate reception of sense impressions and psychological impressions."[26] As Scarry puts it, "at the moment we see something beautiful, we undergo a radical decentering. . . . It is not that we cease to stand at the center of the world, for we never stood there. It is that we cease to stand even at the center of our own world. We willingly cede our ground to the thing that stands before us."[27]

[24] John O'Donahue, *Beauty: The Invisible Embrace* (New York: HarperCollins, 2004), 13.
[25] Scarry, *On Beauty and Being Just*, 112–13.
[26] Ibid., 111.
[27] Ibid., 111–12.

The liberation theologian and ecofeminist Ivone Gebara seems to agree with Scarry, Murdoch, and Weil when she suggests that "beauty can wake us up to care, to enlarge our world, to go beyond our skin, to feel the pleasure of being alive."[28] Like Adler, Gebara notes the self-transcending power of beauty. But like Scarry, she also sees the potential of beauty to draw us beyond our own selfish concerns.

Scarry, though, goes even further, suggesting that the symmetry and balance of beauty prepares us for the notions of equality and justice. In works of beauty there are hints and echoes of justice, suggesting and reminding us of the just society. Scarry argues that the love and reverence of equality in beautiful things prepares the human mind and community to recognize the beauty of equality (and thus justice) in political arrangements.[29]

There is, of course, no guarantee that beauty will unself or decenter us in ways that render us just or compassionate. There are, sadly enough, plenty of villains who savor the splendor of a sunset or create or collect works of beauty and art; and most of those who covet and hoard the world's wealth have a great love for beautiful things—if only to possess them. But Adler, Scarry, Murdoch, and Weil would all agree that humans need the contemplative and self-transcending rest that the enjoyment of beauty can provide, and that a life without any openness to the transcendent or the neighbor is a deeply impoverished existence in which no one should be long enslaved.

The Right to a Sabbath

If Adler and others see the enjoyment of beauty as essential to our humanity because it provides us with a contemplative and self-transcending rest and helps to unself and decenter us, Scripture says something similar about the Sabbath. For though we may normally think of the Sabbath rest as a religious duty or command, the Bible also presents the Sabbath as a liberating gift that helps us achieve our humanity by enjoying a contemplative and self-transcending rest and by turning our attention and concerns outward to the unrecognized neighbor. Indeed, the command to observe a Sabbath rest is also (even primarily?) a command to respect the right of everyone, especially the poor, to enjoy this liberating

---

[28] Ivone Gebara, "Yearning for Beauty," *The Other Side*, 30, no. 4 (2003): 25.
[29] Scarry, *On Beauty and Being Just*, 97–100.

rest. Like the enjoyment of beauty, the Sabbath rest frees us from drudgery by opening us to the transcendent and draws us outside ourselves by turning to the neighbor.

Richard Lowery notes that the first creation narrative in Genesis 1:1–2:4 culminates in the Sabbath rest of the seventh day.[30] According to Lowery, this entire creation account, moving from the chaos and violence of *tohu wabohu* to the peace and harmony of a well-ordered cosmos, reaches its fulfillment in the blessed and holy Sabbath day of rest. Here the Sabbath is not merely an appendix or sequel to the work of creation; it is its fulfillment, its culmination, its completion. The creation of the world and humanity is celebrated *and* completed in and through this Sabbath rest.

This means that the world is not fully created until a Sabbath rest has been incorporated into its ongoing story, until a resting and peaceful breath has been placed in the heart of the universe, a rest that ensures shalom and harmony throughout creation. It also means that humans, fashioned in the image and likeness of their Creator, have not been fully created or become fully human until they have been introduced to the Sabbath rest enjoyed by this Creator and shared with them.

For the humans are not fashioned in the image and likeness of a slave forced to toil "all the days of your life" (cf. Gen 3:17). Instead, they are created in the image of a personal and transcendent Creator with whom they are invited to share this Sabbath rest. And it is in entering into this Sabbath, in being liberated from the daily work of survival to attend to the wondrous, awesome, and transcendent, that their creation as humans reaches its completion. Now, provided with a Sabbath rest that allows them to open themselves to the transcendent and to experience themselves not merely as worker bees but as cocreators of a world of beauty, their own creation is complete. For without the contemplative and self-transcending rest of the Sabbath, without the blessed and holy day that opens them to the transcendent, they are not fully human.

Lowery also notes that a creation that culminates in a Sabbath rest is abundant and bounteous, providing all of God's creatures with more than enough to be fruitful and multiply. In a world with a permanent

---

[30] Richard Lowery, "Sabbath and Survival: Abundance and Self-Restraint in a Culture of Excess," *Encounter* 54, no. 2 (Spring 1993).

Sabbath, six days of labor produce enough food for the entire week. People do not need to struggle every day for survival, because creation is bountiful and the Creator is generous and provident. Within a creation that climaxes with a Sabbath rest there is no need for avarice, coveting, or hoarding, no justification for an endless quest for more or for depriving others of what they need. In the shadow of the Sabbath there is enough for everyone, and everyone has a right to their fair share of creation's abundance.

The Sabbath rest, then, reveals a God who intends that everyone receive what they need from creation's bounty, that none be reduced to bondage or poverty. As Lowery puts it, "Impoverishment and degradation are unnatural in the Sabbath view," for "all people have the right to sufficient food, clothing, housing, safety and dignity."[31] And so the Sabbath rest is an invitation not only to open ourselves to God but also to recognize the humanity of all our neighbors and to share God's bounty with them. The Sabbath is against hoarding, coveting, robbing. It is against poverty, slavery, and starvation. It is meant to open us to both God and the neighbor.

GOD'S DEMAND FOR SABBATH REST IN EXODUS AND DEUTERONOMY

When God sends Moses and Aaron to confront Pharaoh in Exodus 5, the first demand is to release the Hebrews for a few days to go and celebrate a feast for Yahweh. But Pharaoh abhors the very thought of a religious holiday for these teeming slaves, and he imposes crippling and deadly increases in their workload. "What do you mean," he demands of Moses and Aaron, to give these people "rest from their labor?" (Exod 5:4-5; NAB).

Why does Pharaoh react with such violence to this request for a "rest" for his slaves? Surely all slave owners and overseers must give some rest to their slaves, just as they would provide rest for their cattle and oxen; even beasts of burden require sleep and recuperation. And unless an owner seeks to exhaust or destroy his property, he will tend and care for it.

But Pharaoh reacts so violently to this demand for a Sabbath to worship God because *this* rest is a requirement not of chattel or slaves but of free people, of fully human persons. Oxen and asses do not worship. Humans worship. Giving a beast time off to rest weary bones is very

---

[31] Ibid., 163.

different from recognizing a human right to a rest that opens one to the transcendent. And Moses and the Hebrews are demanding that Pharaoh recognize their right to a uniquely human rest, a rest dedicated to worship. This the slave master cannot abide. This rest must be forbidden, for it will (and does) lead inevitably to liberation.

Under Pharaoh the Hebrews live and work as slaves, toiling endlessly and dying early under their merciless overseers. And so Yahweh sends Moses to liberate Israel from this horrible bondage. But that liberation begins with the demand for a rest dedicated to God, a release from mindless and crushing toil through a Sabbath that allows these slaves to worship their Lord and God. And each time Moses and Aaron return to Pharaoh, they repeat the Lord's demand to "let my people go in order to worship me."

Once the Hebrews are liberated from Pharaoh, God demands that these former slaves institute a regular Sabbath rest and extend this rest to all the aliens and slaves in their households. And once the Hebrews have settled in Canaan, this notion of a Sabbath rest that liberates slaves gives birth to the release of slaves and the cancelation of debts every Sabbatical (seventh) year and the redemption of homelands every Jubilee (seventh seventh) year. Growing like wildfire, the notion of Sabbath rest leaps from a three-day pilgrimage into the desert to the release of all the Hebrews from their Egyptian captivity, to a rest for all slaves and aliens, to their ultimate liberation and redemption. No wonder Pharaoh abhorred such an idea. No wonder Jesus claimed the Sabbath was made for humans, and not humans for the Sabbath.

This is the background for God's commandment to "keep holy the Sabbath day," a background that shows, as Patrick Miller argues, that the Sabbath is a divine gift that liberates slaves from bondage by ensuring them a holy and blessed rest dedicated to God and by demanding that this humanizing rest be extended to all the world's slaves and oppressed.[32] As Miller sees it, the Sabbath rest commanded by God in Exodus 20 and Deuteronomy 5 liberates slaves by directing them to a rest "that is open to God" and demands the ongoing liberation of all peoples by directing us to extend this Sabbath to slave and stranger alike. This twin trajectory, opening us up to God and neighbor, is what makes the Sabbath commandment the centerpiece of the Decalogue, directing us to the divine and the other.

---

[32] Patrick D. Miller, "The Human Sabbath: A Study in Deuteronomic Theology," *The Princeton Seminary Bulletin* 6, no. 2 (1985): 86–93.

CATHOLIC SOCIAL TEACHING ON SABBATH

Given Miller's description of the Sabbath as a divine gift that liberates slaves from endless and crippling toil, it seems fitting that the very first Catholic social encyclical, written "to save unfortunate working people from the cruelty of men of greed, who use human beings as mere instruments for money-making,"[33] should list the right to Sabbath rest as the first of workers' rights. When Pope Leo XIII wrote *Rerum Novarum* in 1891, the pope sought to defend workers against the excesses of laissez-faire capitalism at the height of the Industrial Revolution, and he argued that workers had a right to private property, a living wage, and safe working conditions. But at the top of the list of workers' rights came the right to a Sabbath rest. As Leo argued, on the physical level workers have a right to a rest that will prevent them from being worn down and exhausted by their labors. But as spiritual beings they are first entitled to another sort of rest: "A rest from labor [that] is not to be understood as mere giving way to idleness . . . [or] an occasion for spending money and for vicious indulgence, . . . [but] rest from labor, hallowed by religion."[34] As Leo saw it, workers require a rest that would "dispose them to forget for a while the business of everyday life, [and] turn their thoughts to things heavenly, and to the worship which they so strictly owe to the eternal Godhead."[35]

From their various perspectives, Adler, Scarry, Scripture, and Catholic Social Teaching all seem to agree that humans have a fundamental need for more than just bread, clothing, and shelter. Humans, if they are to achieve their full potential and liberation, must also find in their lives some opportunity for a contemplative rest that opens them to the transcendent. They must have some regular release from the oppression of the mundane and practical, or from forced and endless toil. Without such rest they are little more than animated tools (Aristotle's definition of a slave) or beasts of burden. And any real struggle for liberation and justice must have this rest or release as a cornerstone.

At the same time, Scarry, Gebara, and Miller suggest that any genuine rest that opens humans to the transcendent must also lead us to recognize and care for the other. Scarry, Murdoch, Weil, and Gebara believe or hope that beauty can provide this unselfing or decentering rest, while Miller

---

[33] Leo XIII, *Rerum Novarum*, no. 42.
[34] Ibid., no. 41.
[35] Ibid.

and Leo XIII have staked their hopes on a Sabbath rest. Either way, the rest that makes us human must also help us see and respond to the humanity of our neighbor.

If the enjoyment of beauty can provide us with a contemplative and self-transcending rest, and if this same beauty can help to unself and decenter us in ways that help us become more just and compassionate—and thus more humane—then perhaps we have a right to beauty. The God we find in Exodus and Deuteronomy certainly believes that no human should be enslaved in a life without any sacred and holy rest and that all of us should extend this liberating and humanizing rest to all our neighbors. Perhaps that is not so different from saying that the God who fashioned a world of beauty and who created humans in her own image and likeness would not want to see any of her children trapped in a life stripped of all beauty and devoid of any Sabbath.

The Right to Cocreate Beauty

Adler believes that the enjoyment or contemplation of beauty is indispensable for a well-lived life, that humans need beauty for the contemplative rest it provides. But the humans fashioned in the image and likeness of the Creator of a world of beauty are not merely observers and consumers of beauty; they are also cocreators of beauty—or artists. And in *Art in Action* Nicholas Wolterstorff argues that the need and talent to create art or beauty is not the preserve of a small cluster of elite geniuses but a universal human condition. In every age, in every place, no matter how difficult or brutal the conditions, no matter how much energy and resources were required to meet the need to survive, humans have fashioned works of beauty or art. The impulse to create art, to exercise the human calling as cocreators of a world of beauty, is not a luxury but a pervasive and fundamental human need. "We know of no people," Wolterstorff writes, "which has done without music and fiction and poetry and role-playing and sculpture and visual depiction."[36] And we know of no people who merely read, watched, or listened to these works of art without creating and fashioning their own works of beauty.

From Paleolithic cave paintings to the kindergarten masterpieces decorating America's refrigerators, the instinct to create works of beauty is

---

[36] Wolterstorff, *Art in Action*, 4.

timeless and universal. It is not reserved to the small cluster of geniuses who make their living as professional artists, and its product is not to be found only in galleries, museums, concert halls, or theaters. Instead, all humans and every human community has a basic need and talent to create beauty, and all human work should be structured in such a way as to allow people to exercise this talent. For the ability to contribute to the ongoing creation of a world of beauty is an essential human right, which may explain why in 1996 the democratic postapartheid government of South Africa recognized human creativity as a human right and described support for the arts as "a necessary part of good democratic governance."[37] It may also explain why article 27 of the United Nations' Universal Declaration of Human Rights defends not only a right "to enjoy the arts" but also a right "freely to participate in the cultural life of the community."

Few have defended the right to create beauty as clearly or forcefully as William Morris, who decried the way industrial workers of the late nineteenth century were reduced to mere cogs and slaves by a division of labor that prevented them from exercising any creativity or making any real mark upon the fruits of their labor, as well as the way they were constantly pressured by competitive capitalism to produce worthless and ugly objects. Morris railed against the way laborers in England's factories and furnaces were forced to live and work in cities and towns stained and darkened by filth, pollution, and squalor. He argued that all workers had a right to decent living conditions and surroundings, including clean, healthy, and well-built houses, abundant garden spaces in every town, and stretches of wild and unspoiled landscape. But the central claim to which Morris returned again and again was that every worker had a right to work that was fitting, pleasant, and useful—and by this he meant that no one should be forced to produce objects without value, use, and beauty.[38] Work is the central occupation of every person, and that work should, according to Morris, allow persons to make things that are both useful and works of art.

"Time was," Morris argued, "when everybody that made anything made a work of art besides a useful piece of goods, *and it gave them plea-*

[37] John W. de Gruchy, *Christianity, Art and Transformation: Theological Aesthetics in the Struggle for Justice* (New York: Cambridge University Press, 2001), 3.

[38] Morris, "Art, Socialism and Environment," 32–36.

sure to make it." [39] And it was his goal that in a new or renewed age of crafts, this should once again be the case. As Morris saw it, the creativity of art must either be "shared by all people" or abandoned as a sham. It must be "part of the daily life of every man . . . and with us wherever we go" or recognized as a meaningless luxury.[40] Providing all people with fitting and honorable work in which they can take pleasure will extend art to all and make an end of degrading toil.

CREATED AS COCREATORS OF BEAUTY

In different ways both of the creation accounts found in the first chapters of Genesis affirm that *all* persons are called to be creators and tenders of beauty. As we saw above, in Genesis 1:26-27 humans are fashioned in the image and likeness of the Creator of a world of beauty, a Creator who has transformed the violent and chaotic wilderness of *tohu wabohu* into a free and well-ordered cosmos. To be created in the image of this Creator of beauty must mean that humans also have a vocation to be creators of beauty and that they cannot be deprived of this capacity without being in some way violated or diminished. At the same time, we read in Genesis 2:15 that humans have been created and placed in Eden to cultivate and care for the beauty of this lush garden. In this second creation account humans have a vocation as gardeners, tillers, and caretakers of the beauty and bounty of God's creation.

The Universal Catholic Catechism echoes the Bible's description of our human vocation to be cocreators of beauty when it notes that "Created 'in the image of God,' man also expresses the truth of his relationship with God the Creator by the beauty of his artistic works. Indeed, art is a distinctively human form of expression; . . . Arising from talent given by the Creator, . . . art bears a certain likeness to God's activity in what he has created."[41] Or, as Sara Maitland argues in *A Big-Enough God: Artful Theology*, the artistic creativity of humans takes place "in the light of the creative power of our God."[42]

---

[39] William Morris, *Art and the Beauty of the Earth* (London: Longmans & Company, 1898), 13; emphasis added.

[40] Ibid., 16.

[41] *Catechism of the Catholic Church*, 2nd ed. (Washington, DC: United States Catholic Conference, 1994), no. 2501.

[42] Sara Maitland, *A Big-Enough God: Artful Theology* (London: A. R. Mowbray & Company, 1995), 142.

LIBERATED SLAVES BECOME COCREATORS

If Genesis 1–2 makes the case that humans have a vocation to be co-creators of beauty, Exodus shows that all persons have a right to the sort of fitting and pleasant labor Morris demanded for industrial workers—work that allows them to exercise their full creativity as humans and produce works of art. In the essay "Slaves or Sabbath Keepers?" Ellen Davis argues that the key to the Hebrews' liberation from Egypt was their release from the "bad work" of slavery and their taking up of a system of "good work" grounded in the Sabbath; and what distinguished this "good work" from slavery was that it provided the Hebrews with an opportunity to develop and exercise their human freedom and creativity as cocreators.[43]

Like Lowery, Davis argues that the liberation of Israel starts with the call for a brief rest to worship Yahweh (Exod 5) and continues in the Decalogue's permanent institution of a Sabbath rest for all the Hebrews and every member of their households (Exod 20). But Davis goes on to suggest that in Exodus "good" or Sabbath-based work also includes the freedom to participate in the creation and design of works of beauty and the ability to labor in ways that tap into and develop one's full range of talents as cocreators of beauty. Liberated persons and communities do not merely have a right to a Sabbath rest; they also have a right to bring their minds and creativity, along with the sweat of their brow, to the labors they take up.

Under Pharaoh and his overseers, a teeming sea of Hebrew slaves had toiled, suffered, and died in the construction of Egypt's public works, raising up store cities and monuments for generations of pharaohs. Under this regime the Hebrews had already had the "privilege" of helping to build works of beauty. But although the palaces, temples, and fortifications of these Egyptian store cities were drenched in the sweat and blood of countless Hebrew workers, these slaves had not consented to this backbreaking toil and had no hand in the design or planning of the monuments or cities built with the mountains of brick and stone they quarried and carried. The Hebrews had worked on these cities, but not as free people or cocreators of beauty. The plaintive cries Yahweh hears and responds to in Exodus 3 makes it clear the work of these slaves is

---

[43] Ellen Davis, "Slaves or Sabbath-Keepers? A Biblical Perspective on Human Work," *Anglican Theological Review,* 83, no. 1 (Winter 2001): 25–40.

not—by any stretch of the imagination—honorable, fitting, or pleasant.

That would all change with the construction of the tabernacle, a labor of love and beauty the Hebrews would take up, pay for, design, and carry out as a free people. Once safely out of Egypt, the Hebrews receive instructions from Yahweh for the construction of the sacred ark, a tabernacle that will carry the twin tablets of the Decalogue, and a work of unparalleled beauty that will also be *their* first public work. In the construction of the tabernacle—funded by the freewill offerings of liberated slaves, carried out under the wisdom and direction of a Hebrew master builder (Betzalel), and executed with the craft, skill, and wisdom of legions of Hebrew weavers, carpenters, and artisans—a society of slaves is being transformed into a liberated people.

No longer toiling as slaves under Pharaoh's overseers, the Hebrews take up good, honorable, pleasant, and fitting Sabbath-based work that marks them as a free people. As Davis sees it, the thirteen chapters in Exodus given over to the tabernacle project form a matching bookend to the first thirteen chapters describing the Hebrews' release from the "bad work" done under Pharaoh; and the process of learning to work as artisans and master builders is key to the Hebrews' liberation and release from bondage.

WORKERS' RIGHT TO BE COCREATORS OF BEAUTY

Catholic Social Teaching does not explicitly assert or defend the right to be cocreators of beauty, but there is a good deal in its treatment of the meaning and purpose of human work that lends support to the existence of such a right.

Pope John Paul II argues that "human work is *a key*, probably *the essential key*, to the whole social question."[44] And it would be difficult to think of a topic that has occupied modern Catholic Social Teaching more than the meaning and purpose of work and the dignity and rights of workers. At the heart of these reflections has been the belief that humans have a right and a vocation to work and that human work is fundamentally different from the physical labor other creatures perform to sustain their lives because we fulfill and achieve our humanity through this work.

---

[44] John Paul II, *Laborem Exercens*, no. 3; emphasis in original.

As John Paul II puts it, "work is a good thing" for humans, and for our humanity, because through work a person *achieves fulfillment* as a human being and indeed, in a sense, becomes 'more a human being.' "[45] According to the pope, work is a primary means by which we "fulfill the calling to be a person," the way we live out our role of cocreators fashioned in the image and likeness of God.[46]

In Catholic Social Teaching humans work to earn their daily bread and meet the material needs of their families; so all workers have the right to a just wage, safe working conditions, and adequate rest. But, as John Paul II notes above, work is also "a principle way that people exercise the distinctive human capacity for self-expression and self-realization."[47] In our labor we work not just on our workbenches but on ourselves, developing our talents and skills, educating and enriching our hearts and hands and heads, fulfilling our vocation to become fully human persons. And so we need work that allows us to grow and to exercise our full range of human skills and abilities, work that enables us to become artisans and craftsmen. Finally, our work provides us with the means to join with others in building up the common good of the human community, and so we need to be able to participate fully and freely in the economic and political systems and structures that create and sustain our world. We need work that not only provides us with a fair wage, adequate rest, and safe conditions but also offers us a way to participate in and create a better world.

Since human work is meant "for the development of one's powers," the church has recommended "partnership contracts" that allow "workers and executives [to] become sharers in the ownership or management" of companies.[48] And because human work is to be carried out by "free and independent human beings created in the image of God," Catholic Social Teaching has called for the active participation of all workers in the various economic enterprises in which they labor.[49] Indeed, over the years, Catholic Social Teaching has repeatedly called for "new forms of partnership between workers and managers" that "expand economic participation, broaden the sharing of economic power, and make eco-

[45] Ibid., no. 9; emphasis in original.

[46] Ibid., nos. 1 and 6.

[47] National Conference of Catholic Bishops, Economic Justice for All, no. 97. Cf. John Paul II, *Laborem Exercens*, nos. 6 and 10.

[48] Pius XI, *Quadragesimo Anno*, nos. 52 and 65.

[49] Second Vatican Council, *Gaudium et Spes*, no. 68.

nomic decision more accountable to the common good,"[50] while John Paul II has argued that every laborer has the right "to take part in the very work process as a sharer in responsibility and creativity."[51]

All of this implies that Catholic social thought understands work as a distinctively human activity that enables persons to achieve and fulfill their vocation as cocreators fashioned in the image and likeness of the Creator of a word of beauty. Work is not merely the way humans earn their daily bread; it is also (even primarily?) the way they achieve their identity and live out their calling as persons, as well as the means by which they join together freely with other humans to build up that great work of human art—civilization. Human work helps us to become artists and enables us to build our greatest works of beauty; and we have a right to this work and beauty.

Practical examples of the human need and right to be creators of beauty abound. In *What Good Are the Arts?* art scholar and critic John Carey reports on various studies tracking the impact made on prisoners who participate in creative art programs.[52] In study after study, prisoners who were allowed to participate in creative writing, drama, and art classes or projects showed marked improvement in their self-esteem, initiative, creativity, and behavior—improvements, unfortunately, that often disappeared when released prisoners were unable to continue this participation because such programs were not readily available to the poor and the working class.

As Carey sees it, the violence and crime committed by most prisoners is a reflection of and reaction to their experience of powerlessness. Poor, unemployed, and disenfranchised persons turn to violence and crime in large part because they are stripped of power, cut off from the fundamental need to fulfill their potential and make their mark. But when the powerless are provided with an opportunity to express their creativity and to fashion things of beauty, they experience all the pleasures and satisfactions of work that Morris called honorable, fitting, and pleasant, and they find, as John Paul II argued, that such work helps them to "become more of a human being."

And so Carey argues that

---

[50] National Conference of Catholic Bishops, Economic Justice for All, no. 297.

[51] John Paul II, *Laborem Exercens*, no. 15.

[52] John Carey, *What Good Are the Arts?* (New York: Oxford University Press, 2006), 152ff.

every child in every school should have a chance to paint and model and sculpt and sing and dance and act and play every instrument in the orchestra, to see if that is where he or she will find joy and fulfillment and self-respect as many others have found it. Of course it will be expensive—very, very expensive. But then, so are prisons. Perhaps if more money had been spent on, more imagination and effort devoted to, more government initiative directed towards art in schools and art in the community, Britain's prisons would not now be so overcrowded.[53]

This grand proposal will strike many as hopelessly naïve and idealistic, particularly in an age when so many of America's urban and rural schools fail to provide our nation's poor with a basic education in reading and math. But since 1975, Venezuelan economist, musician, and educator Antonio Abreu has acted as if every child in his nation—especially the poor—is entitled to be a creator of beauty. For well over three decades, Abreu has directed the National System of Youth and Children's Orchestras (known as *el sistema*), which incorporates over a quarter of a million young, largely poor Venezuelans between the ages of two and eighteen into 220 youth orchestras and 60 children's orchestras.[54]

In 246 centers (*nucleos*) scattered throughout Venezuela, 270,000 children and youth practice classical music two to three hours a day, learning to play in orchestras almost from the start and forming a social movement "credited with improving the lives of young people who might otherwise have been drawn into lives of crime and drug abuse."[55] Indeed, studies by the Inter-American Development Bank, which has loaned Abreu $155 million to build eight regional *el sistema* centers, show some of the benefits experienced by the two million mostly poor Venezuelan youth who have learned to play great works of art with other children. School dropout rates decline significantly among these children, as do rates for crime, drug use, and juvenile delinquency.[56]

And Abreu's faith in young people's right to create beauty seems to be contagious. The Los Angeles Philharmonic is set to inaugurate a Youth Orchestra L.A., with the ultimate aim of providing every child—espe-

[53] Ibid., 167.

[54] Arthur Lublow, "Conductor of the People," *New York Times Magazine*, October 28, 2007, 32–37.

[55] Press release, "Dr. Jose Antonio Abreu Awarded Coveted 2008 Glenn Gould Prize," Glenn Gould Foundation, Toronto, February 14, 2008.

[56] Ibid., 34.

cially the poor—in Los Angeles County with a place in a youth or child orchestra. And the Chicago and Boston symphonies are planning similar initiatives, while a number of Latin American and the Caribbean nations have already instituted their own versions of *el sistema*.[57] A right to create beauty, it seems, is not an outlandish notion.

The Right to a Fair Share of Creation's Bounty

The Ugliness of Injustice

Beauty is not always a sign of justice, as objects of great beauty can hide terrible iniquity. Splendid monuments, temples, and palaces have often been built with the forced labor of slaves and financed with crushing taxes and tolls extorted from the poor; gorgeous estates and mansions of the wealthy have been frequently paid for with unjust profits, stolen wages, and usurious interest rates. Isaiah, Jeremiah, and Amos railed against the exquisite summer and winter homes of the wealthy, condemned their lavish estates decorated with terraces and gardens, and reviled their spacious apartments inlaid with ivory, paneled with cedar, and painted with vermillion—not because they despised their architectural splendor, but because these beautiful homes were stolen from the poor and financed with fraud, unjust levies, and unpaid labor.[58] As Isaiah 3:14 notes, "In your houses are the spoils taken from the poor."

In the view of these prophets, the iniquity, corruption, and violence that built these mansions and estates have rendered them hideous and grotesque because, although it may often wear a mask of beauty, injustice itself is always ugly and mars the world and all it touches with its ugliness. This is what Pires da Silveira means when he says that hunger, poverty, disease, wars, drugs, and violence are ugly and dirty and make our world ugly and dirty.[59] It is what John de Gruchy means when he notes that apartheid "was not only unjust but also ugly."[60] It is the truth we know when we see photographs of slums, ghettos, and barrios; when we look upon the skeletal figures hanging on to concentration camp

---

[57] Greg Sandow, "What Classical Music Should Be," *The Wall Street Journal*, December 13, 2007, D6.

[58] Amos 3:15; 5:11; Jer 22:13-15; Isa 3:14-15; 5:8-9.

[59] Pires da Silveira, "Justice, Bread and Beauty," 103.

[60] De Gruchy, *Christianity, Art and Transformation*, 1.

fences or being herded into refugee camps and settlements; when we see the faces of children toiling in sweat shops, sold into brothels, or recruited by warlords. It is the truth that injustice is ugly.

Indeed, the ugliness of injustice has long been a theme of social critics and reformers. In novels like *Hard Times* and *The Jungle*, reform-minded writers like Charles Dickens and muckraking journalists like Upton Sinclair reached for their readers' hearts by trying to capture the filth and squalor in which industrial workers tried to eke out a living. Meanwhile, in works like *Street Life in London* and *How the Other Half Lives*, early photojournalists like John Thomson and Jacob Riis brought their audiences face to face with the brutal ugliness of poverty and injustice. In the decades that followed, the photographer Lewis Hine scalded a nation's conscience with pictures of the piteous squalor in which millions of our country's immigrants and children toiled, and in works like *An American Exodus: A Record of Human Erosion*, the great documentary photographer Dorothea Lange served up haunting images of the faces of exploited sharecroppers, displaced farmers, and migrant workers.[61] In our own time, the Brazilian economist turned photojournalist Sebastiao Salgado has held up the scarred and disfigured faces and bodies of injustice, avarice, and oppression in books like *Workers: An Archeology of the Industrial Age* and *Terra: Struggles of the Landless*; and in books like *Rachel and Her Children* and *Amazing Grace*, the teacher and activist Jonathan Kozol has introduced his readers to the ugliness created by discrimination, unemployment, homelessness, and poverty.[62] In all these works, injustice is not merely an abstract and academic principle but a filthy, crowded tenement under a leaden sky of poisoned smoke, or the exhausted blackened face of a miner or factory worker who should have been in school.

The ugliness of injustice has two faces. First, we see the grotesque and dreadful conditions in which the world's poor and oppressed live and work, as well as the awful disfigurement and scarring suffered by the countless victims of greed, hatred, and violence. Injustice has marred and stained the overcrowded, polluted, and exhausted places where

---

[61] Dorothea Lange, *An American Exodus: A Record of Human Erosion* (Paris: Editions Jean-Michel Place, 2000 [1939]).

[62] Sebastiao Slagado, *Workers: An Archeology of the Industrial Age* (New York: Aperture, 2005), and *Terra: Struggles of the Landless* (London: Phaidon Press, 1998); Jonathan Kozol, *Rachel and Her Children: Homeless Families in America* (New York: Three Rivers Press, 2006), and *Amazing Grace* (New York: Harper Perennial, 1996).

these forgotten and invisible neighbors try to scratch out their daily crust or crumbs, marking them with a gruesome ugliness. And it has tattooed the hungry, tired, desperate, filthy bodies of these same neighbors with a similar ugliness, marking their eyes with fear and their flesh with every manner of sore, blemish, and scar.

And, second, we see the ugliness of a world thrown off balance by a growing divide between the haves and the have-nots. If beauty is a matter of symmetry, balance, and harmony, the ugliness of injustice is to be found in the picture of two very separate and radically unequal worlds, in the grotesque greed with which so many of us in the first world hoard and consume far more than our fair share of the bounty of creation while billions of our neighbors scrape by on less than a few dollars a day.

A few years ago the Holocaust museum in Washington, DC, came into possession of a collection of photographs illustrating the domestic and private lives of administrators and staff at Auschwitz.[63] Black-and-white snapshots show smiling clerical workers and military personnel relaxing and singing together, lighting a Christmas tree, eating bowls of fresh blueberries, and enjoying a staff picnic. Without the context of the horror going on just yards away from these idyllic scenes, these photos would look charming and sweet. But knowing what we do about Auschwitz and the other death camps, the pictures evoke an indescribable ugliness. They are an abomination.

So, too, the ugliness of injustice is not simply the ugliness of the degrading squalor in which the poor and oppressed are forced to live. It is also the ugliness of the juxtaposition of this squalor with the splendor of so much conspicuous and unconscionable wealth and consumption. The ugliness of injustice is that it is two-faced and that in an unjust world billions have been robbed of their fair (beautiful and just) share of the bounty of creation.

A "FAT" AND BOUNTEOUS CREATION

In the Sabbath creation narrative of Genesis 1:1–2:4, God has fashioned a world that is "fat." According to Richard Lowery, the verb used in this account to describe God's creative activity also means to fatten or make fat, and it suggests a creation that is abundant, ample, and plentiful, a

---

[63] Neil A. Lewis, "In the Shadow of Horror, SS Guardians Relax and Frolic," *New York Times*, September 19, 2007, E1.

bounteous and overflowing creation where there is enough food and habitat for all God's creatures to be fruitful and multiply.[64] In this fat world there is plenty enough for everyone, enough for all to rest one day out of seven and still be amply taken care of. In this fat world there is no need or justification for hoarding or coveting or stealing or cheating; there is no reason to take someone else's fair share or to hunger for more than we need. Instead, the fatness of creation reflects God's gracious and generous will to take care of all creatures, great and small.[65]

For this fat creation points to a God who intends a world that is rich, abundant, and delightful, a world where all God's creatures enjoy the fat bounty of creation and delight in its overflowing abundance. In this fat creation all creatures are to teem and flourish, to be fruitful and multiply, to enjoy. Indeed, the beauty of this creation *is* its fatness, its abundance, its ample provision for all. And in this creation narrative God clearly intends that all creatures shall benefit from and enjoy this beauty, this fatness, and that all shall have a fair (beautiful and just) share of this bounty. As Lowery notes, the command to share creation's bounty "grows out of the assurance that God provides sustenance and beauty sufficient for a good life."[66] Anything else—any coveting, hoarding, cheating, or stealing—would be an affront to the beauty of this creation and its Creator.

We find echoes of this fat creation in the manna story of Exodus 16 and in the six accounts of the multiplication of loaves in the four gospels. In each of these tales, people are frightened that there will not be enough, that God's bounty will be insufficient, that they will need to hoard what they have and to covet what they do not. But the lesson of the manna and the loaves and fishes is that in God's creation there is an ample bounty to be shared with all, a fatness that will provide for all if it is not hoarded, if there is no coveting, cheating, or stealing. In the fat economy of God's creation, six days of collecting will provide enough to feed everyone for the whole week. In this fat economy those who share will find they have an embarrassment of leftovers.

A "Fat" Land of Milk and Honey

And if God's creation is fat and bounteous, so too is the land to which Yahweh promises to deliver the Hebrews. Again and again in Exodus,

---

[64] Lowery, "Sabbath and Survival," 147.
[65] Ibid., 147–48.
[66] Ibid., 162.

Leviticus, Numbers, Deuteronomy, and Joshua, we hear of God's promise to liberate the Hebrews from slavery by bringing them to "a fine, broad land, a land flowing with milk and honey" (Exod 3:8). This Promised Land is, Ezekiel 20:6 tells us, "the most beautiful of all lands" (NIV) and its beauty, like the beauty of creation, flows from its fatness, from its bounty, from God's gracious will to provide for all who dwell there.

For in this fat Promised Land, we read in Deuteronomy 15:4-6, God will bless the Hebrews abundantly, and there will be no poor in their midst. No one will be in need. No one will be driven into borrowing, debt, or servitude, and no foreign kings will conquer or rule over them.

But keeping the promise of this fat land means keeping God's laws—and at the heart of these laws is a commitment to provide everyone with a fair share or portion (*nahalah*) of this land's bounty.[67] And so God directs the Hebrews to provide every tribe and family with a fair parcel of land, forbids the coveting or stealing of anyone else's lands, and ensures that those who lose their homes or liberty through poverty and debt will have their lands and freedom restored in the Sabbatical and Jubilee years. In a similar fashion God commands that the poor be protected from predatory loans, that the hungry be allowed to glean from the crops and vines of their neighbors, and that a tithe be collected for widows, orphans, and poor strangers.

In all of these practices is a commitment to provide everyone with a fair share of the bounty of this "most beautiful of all lands" and to ensure that the weak and powerless, who are most likely to be robbed of their fair portion and allotment, are protected. This is the meaning of the fat land promised the Hebrews: that milk and honey will flow for all.

Ugly Coveting

And yet there is a craving in the human heart, and especially in the hearts of the rich and powerful, that threatens to undo the beauty of the Promised Land, to unmake the bounty of "the most beautiful of all lands." This craving is the appetite to hoard, to acquire more and more possessions, property, and wealth, and to rob or cheat others out of their fair share. [68] Rebelling against God's intent to provide everyone with a

---

[67] Tim Gorringe, *A Theology of the Built Environment* (New York: Cambridge University Press, 2002), 55–57.

[68] Patrick D. Miller, "Property and Possession in Light of the Ten Commandments," in *Having Property and Possession in Religious and Social Life*, ed. William Schweiker and Charles Matthewes (Grand Rapids, MI: Eerdmans, 2004), 42–46.

fair portion of the Promised Land's bounty are hearts that covet the lands and possessions of their neighbors.

The prophets rail against this lust for more, this sick addiction that has the wealthy dreaming up ever-new schemes to defraud and rob the poor of their homes and daily bread. "Woe betide those," Micah 2:1-2 warns, "who lie in bed planning evil and wicked deeds. . . . They covet fields, and take them by force; if they want a house they seize it; they lay hands on both householder and house."

This bottomless greed transforms the rich into vampires, living off the honest sweat of the poor and consuming their neighbors' lands and resources like a plague. Isaiah 5:8 condemns the wealthy for their insatiable appetite for more and more estates, adding house to house and field to field until they have driven everyone else off the land. Amos 8:4-6 complains that the rich cannot wait for the Sabbath to be over so that they can defraud and exploit the poor in the marketplace or sell their neighbors into bondage for the price of a pair of sandals. By fixing their scales, imposing cruel levies, withholding just wages, and defrauding their neighbors in court, the rich are robbing their neighbors blind.

This coveting by the rich is also unmaking the fatness and beauty of the Promised Land, transforming Canaan into a new Egypt, where the poor have been driven off their lands and sold into bondage. In the land made by coveting, the poor, homeless, and enslaved are now legion, and all but a few are trapped in need and imprisoned in debt. The rich are making a wilderness of the Promised Land.

And so the prophets warn that this greed will bring about the destruction of the land, that the palaces and estates of the wealthy will be vacant and barren monuments to their avarice and injustice, that no one will live in these homes or harvest crops from these vineyards and fields, that the rich will be stripped of all their beautiful possessions and decorations, and that famine and pestilence and drought and death will disfigure and scar the land and its people.[69]

All of this is to say that the God who creates a fat world of beauty in Genesis 1:1–2:4 and who liberates the Hebrews from bondage by bringing them to a fat land flowing with milk and honey intends that everyone enjoy a fair share of the bounty of creation and the Promised Land, and commands us to tend and care for the fat beauty of creation and the Promised Land by providing that fair portion to all.

---

[69] See Amos 5:11-12; Isa 3:1-26.

The Beauty of the Fair City

In *The Culture of Cities* and *The City in History*, the renowned historian and architectural critic Lewis Mumford claims that cities are (along with language) humanity's greatest work of art and that the purpose of cities is to humanize us.[70] These twin claims are related. For if cities are a corporate work of art, we should expect them to have some beauty; and one certain way in which they might humanize and civilize us would be to nourish us with different forms of beauty.

To call a city a work of art is not to say that we can expect the same exquisite beauty from a cityscape that we might encounter hanging on the walls of the Metropolitan Museum of Art or the Louvre. No real municipality or neighborhood will be as radiant as a series of Monet haystacks or as glorious as a Van Gogh wheat field. We do not expect to be swept up in aesthetic ecstasy when we step out our doors and walk down the street to the corner shop, or when we arrive at work after a long commute from the suburbs. But it is reasonable to suggest that cities and towns should provide all their citizens and visitors with some minimal spiritual nourishment from their surroundings. We have the right to expect that our cities will not be filthy, depressing, enervating, and dreary. We have some right to hope that the places where over half the planet's population now lives and works will not be marked by unrelieved tedium, soul-sucking sameness, and endless ugliness. That seems like the least we can expect from something Mumford called our greatest work of art.

The claim that cities humanize us goes back to Aristotle, who argues that cities are the places where we learn to work and play with others, where we acquire and develop the virtues required to collaborate with friends and strangers in the construction of a rich and diverse community.[71] Cities pull us beyond family and tribe and force us to cooperate with strangers and aliens in the great work of forging a dynamic and integrated society. This seems like another way of saying that cities teach us justice, or that in the labor of creating a vibrant and life giving city we learn to be just.

At the same time, cities humanize us by providing us with the basic goods and services needed to flourish as human beings. Cities civilize

---

[70] Lewis Mumford, *The Culture of Cities* (London: Secker and Warburger, 1938), 5; Lewis Mumford, *The City in History* (Harmondsworth: Penguin, 1991 [1961]), 127.

[71] Gorringe makes this argument in *A Theology of the Built Environment*, 147.

us by offering their citizens what is required for a good life, what we need to develop our potential as persons and members of society. And, as Tim Gorringe argues in *A Theology of the Built Environment*, one of the things the humanizing city must provide is beauty.[72] Not always an ecstatic and sublime beauty, but at least enough beauty to keep us from shriveling up and dying.

Cities need to provide us with beauty because the architecture of our neighborhoods and cities, the built urban environment in which over half of us now live, is a third human skin that we inhabit and inhale. Architecture is the art in which we live and breathe, the art that stands over and around us, the art we were born into and within which we work, play, sleep, and pray, the art that has sunk so deeply into our consciousness we usually forget it is there.[73] And just as fish need the clean water they do not notice and mammals need the fresh air they cannot see, so humans need a third skin touched with some beauty.

We are incarnate beings—embodied spirits—and the environment and habitat in which our bodies live and work is critical to us and shapes who we are and who we become. We are deeply and unconsciously affected by the larger architecture of our lives, shaped by the moral messages and principles embodied in the built environment of our homes, neighborhoods, and cities, and diminished by settings that have been stripped of beauty, dignity, and honor. As Muley Graves argues in John Steinbeck's *Grapes of Wrath*, the "place where folks live is them folks,"[74] and folks need beauty.

Ivone Gebara understands the need for cities that provide us with beauty. "From Genesis," she writes, "we know that beauty is our birthright." But a beauty stripped of justice "is false, a facade," and cities that provide only monuments and palaces for the elite are such ugly facades. Instead, "well-kept neighborhoods, clean streets, and good water are essentials for a healthy life" and fundamental elements of the beauty we require from our environment. "If justice is fundamentally about right relationships, beauty is in many ways the incarnation and measure of the integrity of those relationships."[75]

Gorringe agrees with Gebara (and Lewis Mumford and William Morris) that we need clean, healthy, well-lit cities that provide us with ample

---

[72] Ibid., 200–201.
[73] Ibid., 82.
[74] John Steinbeck, *The Grapes of Wrath* (New York: Penguin, 2002), 52.
[75] Gebara, "Yearning for Beauty," 25.

sunlight, fresh air, and clean water, as well as adequate privacy, ample common space, decent housing, and enough green and garden places to relax and renew ourselves. In particular, Gorringe argues that the poor of these cities must have access to beauty. "Almost every human settlement above the hunter gatherer level has its rich and poor, but not every settlement condemns the poor to squalid or inhuman living conditions. How can that be beautiful which fails to respect the image of God?"[76]

Unfortunately, many cities—and large parts of many more cities—are not humanizing works of art, for they fail to provide even a modicum of beauty for their millions and tens of millions of residents, or they exile teeming masses of the poor to barren and toxic urban wastelands of heartbreaking ugliness. In the nineteenth and twentieth centuries, industrialization created filthy, congested, and dangerous urban landscapes overcrowded with millions of tenement dwellers and overshadowed by thousands of belching smokestacks. And since World War II, the hearts of most American cities have been eviscerated by the automobile and suburban sprawl, and the national landscape has been recreated in the image and likeness of the car, leaving us with a dehumanized environment sized for our machines, not for us.

James Howard Kunstler captures the soulless ugliness of much of our nation's current built environment in *The Geography of Nowhere*, noting that

> eighty percent of everything ever built in America has been built in the last 50 years, and most of it is depressing, brutal, ugly, unhealthy and spiritually degrading: the jive-plastic commuter tract home wastelands, the Potemkin village shopping plazas with their vast parking lagoons, the Lego-block hotel complexes, the "gourmet mansardic" junk-food joints, the Orwellian office "parks" featuring buildings sheathed in the same reflective glass as the sunglasses worn by chain-gang guards, the particle-board garden apartments rising up in every meadow and cornfield, the freeway loops around every big and little city with their clusters of discount merchandise marts, the whole destructive, wasteful, toxic, agoraphobia-inducing spectacle that politicians proudly call "growth."[77]

[76] Gorringe, *A Theology of the Built Environment*, 220.

[77] John Howard Kunstler, *The Geography of Nowhere* (New York: Simon and Schuster, 1993), 10.

If cities are to be works of art that humanize us—they must be able to provide all their citizens, rich and poor, with some beauty that nourishes and sustains the human spirit. This need not be the ecstatic and sublime beauty of great works of art, though there is no good reason to fail to provide our nation's poor and underprivileged with access to our greatest paintings, sculpture, and music. But it does mean that in the midst of the one art—architecture—in which we all live and breathe and work, the one art no one can escape being shaped by, everyone should have access to some humanizing and nurturing beauty. Anything else would be a kind of sin against the Creator and all creation.

The Poor's Special Claim to Beauty

The two creation accounts of Genesis 1–2 present beauty as a universal vocation and right. In these stories every human person has a calling and a right to share in the beauty of creation's bounty. But in Exodus, God sends Moses to bring the beauty of the Sabbath and the Promised Land to the poor, landless, and enslaved Hebrews. It is the cries of the poor that have moved Yahweh to send these liberating gifts of beauty, to offer a nation of slaves a Sabbath rest, and to provide a tribe of widows, orphans, and aliens with a land flowing with milk and honey.

In Scripture the poor have a special claim on beauty because they have been stripped and starved of their fair share of creation's fat bounty and their beauty has been stolen. This is why the offer of a Sabbath rest comes first to a nation of impoverished slaves, and why "the most beautiful of lands" is offered to a race of widows, orphans, and aliens. It may also be why God has the Egyptians hand over their gold and silver jewelry and fine garments to these freed slaves (Exod 12:35-36), or why God later demands that all Hebrews setting free an indebted slave should "not let him go empty-handed. Give to him lavishly from your flock, from your threshing-floor and your winepress. Be generous to him as the LORD God has blessed you" (Deut 15:13-15).

In Exodus and the Prophets, the theft of the poor's fair share has unmade the world of beauty fashioned by the Creator and scarred and disfigured the faces of God's little ones, the *anawim*. Those who have robbed the poor savor the splendor of their fine mansions and lush estates, but underneath this cosmetic facade is a seething and violent ugliness that will destroy everything. Their insatiable appetites have stripped the land bare, while their theft of the poor's share of creation has divided the world into hostile camps of haves and have-nots. Only a liberating justice that redeems the poor by restoring their fair share of beauty will undo this ugliness.

The poor have a special claim upon beauty for two reasons: because they are mired in so much ugliness and because they have created so much of the world's beauty. Their first claim to beauty comes from the fact that they have been robbed of their fair share of creation's beauty and forced to live and work in the ugliness created and deepened by this theft. Their second claim arises from the fact that their sweat and sacrifice has created so much of the very beauty from which they are excluded.

The Ugliness of Poverty

The dignity, humanity, and inner beauty of the poor are captured in paintings like Millet's *The Gleaners* or photographs like Dorothea Lange's *Migrant Mother*; but these pictures cannot undo the awful truth that poverty itself is ugly and that the poor are forced to live and work in a horrible ugliness. As Gutierrez noted, the world's poor have been exiled to its rubbish heaps.

If beauty is that which pleases upon being seen, then the poor see little beauty, for their view is crowded with the unpleasant face of want. In place of a fat bounty that will satisfy our needs, the poor see only a collection of desperate hungers that will not go away and cannot be met. There is not enough food, water, clothing, shelter, work, or medicine—and not enough money to pay for any of these. And these hungers and shortages scar and disfigure their surroundings and environments. Streets and alleys in their barrios, ghettos, and slums are dark, filthy, and dangerous, littered with uncollected trash, car wrecks, and potholes. Houses and storefronts are boarded up and windows and street lamps shattered. Schools and grocery stores are fortified like prisons. These overcrowded, polluted, dangerous, and exhausted places are not beautiful. Instead, they are the places shunned by anyone who has access to beauty.

The view of the poor is also crowded with the unpleasant humiliation of being unable to provide for oneself and one's family, and with the ugly scorn of those who see them as miserable freeloaders and failures. The "normal" people we watch on our television sets are all able to get jobs, pay the rent, feed their families, and even send their children to college. But millions of the poor find themselves in a world where these simple tasks are herculean or impossible and where their inability to meet these challenges is a constant source of shame, pity, and disgust.

And when they do find employment, it is the poor who are assigned the work that is dirty and ugly. It is the poor who are expected to pick up and empty our trash, pull our weeds, pluck our chickens, slaughter and butcher our meat, pick our strawberries, change and wash our dirty laundry, mop our floors, scrub our toilets, and clean the diapers of our children and grandparents. If there is a dirty, messy, filthy job to be done, there is certainly a poor person—most likely an immigrant or woman of color—ready to do it.[78] For decades our middle class has moved away from jobs that brought us into contact with dirt, waste, filth, or ugliness; we send someone else's children into our kitchens, dining rooms, bathrooms, basements, and backyards to do our housekeeping. We are a society that creates more waste and trash than any the world has ever seen, and we outsource the cleaning of our growing rubbish heap to the poor.

But we do not simply ask the poor to clean our trash. We also dump our trash and waste and toxins in the very neighborhoods and communities where the poor and minorities live. Around the nation and the planet, middle- and upper-class communities export and dump their refuse and filth to poor and minority communities. For over twenty years, repeated studies have shown that poor and minority communities are twice as likely as their white counterparts to have abandoned toxic waste sites, hazardous waste landfills, garbage dumps, and incinerators.[79] And these same poor communities receive much less protection and help when it comes to safeguarding them from the effects of all this waste or helping them clean up toxic sites and landfills. Not surprisingly, the neighborhoods of the poor and minorities suffer from much more environmental pollution and degradation.

[78] Christine Firer Hinze, "Dirt and Economic Inequality: A Christian-Ethical Peek under the Rug," *The Annual of the Society of Christian Ethics* 21 (2001): 45–62.

[79] Vernice D. Miller, "Building on Our Past, Planning for Our Future," in *Toxic Struggles: The Theory and Practice of Environmental Justice*, ed. Richard Hofrichter (Philadelphia, PA: New Society Publishers, 1993), 128; Robert D. Bullard, "Anatomy of Environmental Racism and the Environmental Justice Movement," in *Confronting Environmental Racism: Voices from the Grassroots*, ed. Robert D. Bullard (Boston, MA: South End Press, 1993), 19; Aaron Sachs, *Eco-Justice: Linking Human Rights and the Environment*, Worldwatch Paper 127 (Washington, DC: Worldwatch Institute, 1995), 10; Benjamin Goldman and Laura Fitton, *Toxic Wastes and Race Revisited: An Update of the 1987 Report on the Racial and Socioeconomic Characteristics of Communities with Hazardous Waste Sites* (Washington, DC: Center for Policy Alternatives, 1994), executive summary.

We also export our toxins and pollution overseas to poor nations, adding to the ugliness of their poverty. As industrial and postindustrial nations in North America and Europe have tightened their environmental controls on manufacturing, mining, and agriculture, they have often shipped pesticides, toxic waste, and "dirty industries" overseas to less developed countries in desperate need of cash but without any resources to protect their citizens from the long-term damage of these hazardous materials. Often enough entire factories have been dismantled, shipped to poorer nations, and reassembled without any new safeguards being installed or implemented.

And what is both tragic and ironic is that this ugliness and poverty fuel more and more poverty and ugliness. For poverty itself is a major source of the environmental degradation threatening to unmake the beauty of creation's bounty, because the desperate needs of the poor make them poor and imprudent stewards of creation. In a world with a burgeoning gap between rich and poor, the world's wealthy consume an ever-more disproportionate share of creation's bounty while billions of poor people are forced to live and work in increasingly overcrowded, polluted, and exhausted places. As a result, those trapped in poverty put greater and greater stress on their overtaxed environments, burning down forests, exhausting topsoil, emptying aquifers, and polluting air in a desperate struggle to meet their day-to-day needs.

And it is, of course, the poor who bear the main brunt of all this environmental degradation. As the United States Catholic bishops argue in their 1991 statement on environmental justice, "The whole human race suffers as a result of environmental blight, and generations yet unborn will bear the cost for our failure to act today. But in most countries today, including our own, it is the poor and the powerless who most directly bear the burden of current environmental carelessness."[80]

In Exodus 3 the terrible cries of the poor drive Yahweh to liberate the Hebrews with the beauty of the Sabbath and the Promised Land. Today billions of the world's poor cry out as well for some share of creation's beauty, and both the ugliness of their poverty and the ugliness dumped upon them because they are poor and powerless should press us to ensure that they receive some fair share of creation's bounty.

---

[80] United States Catholic Conference, Renewing the Earth: An Invitation to Reflection and Action on the Environment in Light of Catholic Social Teaching, I.B.

So Much Beauty Is Made by the Poor

Genesis reports that the beauty of creation was fashioned by God. But history tells us that the great public works of civilization were built by the poor, even though these palaces, temples, monuments, gardens, and squares bear the names of emperors, pharaohs, kings, and pontiffs. In Egypt, Greece, and Rome and throughout the ancient world the labor that quarried and carried the stones or made and laid the bricks was done by legions of long-forgotten peasants and slaves whose names are not recorded in any archway or carved on any pilaster. Without these poor laborers there would be no Pyramids, no Parthenon, no Pantheon. When rulers and regents decided to build their ancient wonders and walls, it was always the poor whose sweat and brawn turned mud to bricks, cut down timber, and raised up columns. In 1 Kings 5–7 we read how Solomon built and furnished the temple and palace named after him, but surely the thirty thousand conscripts assigned to this labor did most of the heavy lifting.

Likewise, much of the beauty and wealth of the modern world owes its existence to the labor and sweat of the poor. At the height of the Industrial Revolution, Leo XIII argued that the wealth and bounty of nations was created by the labor of the working class, and a century later John Paul II argued that all the capital amassed by modern economies was in fact the fruit of countless generations of human labor, most of it done, no doubt, by the poor and the working class.[81] Imagine any great nation or any great public work or monument, and wonder for a moment what would remain if the sweat and labor of the poor and the working class were removed. What city, what monument, what cathedral, what garden, what boulevard was created without the labor of the poor?

And when we turn to personal artifacts of beauty, where would we be without the poor? How many of the roses and floral arrangements that decorate American and European tables are grown in Africa and Central America, tended, pruned, and fertilized by people who could never afford such an arrangement for their own homes?[82] How many suburban lawns and public gardens are tended by immigrant workers who live with six to ten other people in a single apartment? How much of the high-fashion clothing sported on America's runways is stitched

[81] Leo XIII, *Rerum Novarum*, no. 34; John Paul II, *Laborem Exercens*, no. 12.

[82] Ginger Thompson, "Behind Roses' Beauty, Poor and Ill Workers," *New York Times*, February 13, 2003, A1.

together in sweatshops scattered between Southeast Asia and Central America? How much of the gold jewelry adorning middle-class fingers and necks was mined by African and South American laborers living on the edge of poverty? How many of the diamonds decorating our rings and necklaces were dug up by workers who could never afford such adornments for their wives and daughters? And just how lovely would all of our hotel rooms and ballrooms and banquet halls be without the legions of poor workers cleaning, clearing, and decorating all those welcoming spaces?

Indeed, how many great paintings or sculptures would be left if we stripped all our museums of the works done by poor artists? How impoverished would modern art have been if it had not been able to draw inspiration from the work of African tribal artists and other indigenous potters, sculptors, and artisans? Or how would classical music be different if great composers did not feel free to borrow tunes and melodies from peasant folk songs? Or where would contemporary music be if international artists were not appropriating the rhythms and tunes of indigenous peoples? And what about musical art forms like jazz, gospel, and the blues? Where did these great works of beauty come from if not from the poor?

So much of all the beauty created and recreated by human hands has been brought into the world and tended by the sweat and genius of the poor. In ancient Egypt anonymous and illiterate slaves would often put their individual mark on the bricks they made to let someone know they had been there, that a human had made this thing. If we look or listen closely to the many works of beauty in our world, we can see the mark and hear the sound of the poor. "We made, built, carved, fashioned, birthed this work of art," the poor cry, "and we have a claim upon it."

Conclusion

Beauty is not a luxury but a fundamental human calling and right; and all people have a need and a right to enjoy and create beauty. Genesis 1–2 reports that we are made in the image of the Creator of a world of beauty and called to be cocreators and tenders of that beauty and to have a fair share of that beauty. Exodus suggests that our full liberation from slavery demands that we savor and share a contemplative and self-transcending rest that opens us to God and our neighbor, and that we become cocreators of a land made beautiful and bounteous by the justice of God. Scripture makes it clear that beauty is for everyone and that the liberation of the poor demands that their fair share of this beauty be redeemed and returned to them. We should not, to paraphrase Deuteronomy 15:13, send them away empty-handed.

Chapter 3

The Beautiful Stranger: Fashioned in the Image and Likeness of God

This one at last is bone from my bones, flesh from my flesh.

—Genesis 2:23

The Beautiful Neighbor: *Imago Hominis*

What makes us human? The author of the second creation account in Genesis 2 believes it is our ability to recognize and respond to the humanity of others. We become human in the moment we see that the stranger before us is human and shares our humanity, that this alien is our neighbor.

In Carlo Collodi's classic fairy tale, Pinocchio the wooden puppet finally becomes a real boy when he learns to see and care for Geppetto, his beloved papa.[1] His newfound ability to recognize and respond to the stranger as a neighbor and to love this neighbor as (or better than) he loves himself transforms Collodi's wooden tyke into flesh and blood.

---

[1] Carlo Collodi, *Pinocchio*, trans. Geoffrey Brock (New York: NYRB Classics, 2008), 153–60.

And in Genesis 2:23 the clay creature who has been formed of the earth "becomes human" in the moment Adam recognizes and responds to the humanity of Eve, a *shared* humanity that unites them as neighbors.

The woman who stands before Adam in this instant is quite different from him, as every other human and stranger is different from each of us; but Adam also sees and joyfully acknowledges that she is profoundly like him, that they are connected, that she is of his flesh and blood. And in this act of recognizing and responding to her humanity, a shared humanity that binds him to her and to every other stranger he will ever encounter, Adam becomes human.

Indeed, they *both* become human in this moment of mutual recognition, even though, as is often the case in patriarchal societies, we only hear his voice. For surely she too sees a stranger who is different from her, an other who is in many ways *not* like her. But she likewise recognizes and responds to a shared humanity that ties them to one another and that will connect them with all the strangers and others they encounter. Here too is bone of her bones and flesh of her flesh. In this moment the creation of the humans is complete.

In Genesis 2:7 God forms a living creature from the dust of the earth, breathing life into his nostrils, and in 2:15-16 the Lord God places this creature in Eden, providing him with work, shelter, and sustenance. But the creation of the human is not finished. "It is not good for the man to be alone," the Lord God complains in 2:18. The creature who is "alone" is not yet fully formed, not yet fully human. He is radically incomplete. And so God fashions all sorts of animals to keep the creature company, but none of them overcomes this aloneness, none of them completes the creation of the human. So God fashions a second living creature from the rib of the first and presents this woman to the man.

But even the fashioning and presenting of the woman does not in itself complete the creation of the humans or overcome the "aloneness" of the creature. The creatures must choose to become human. They must reach out of their "aloneness" and recognize and respond to the humanity of the other. They must acknowledge that the other is a neighbor and friend. They must care about what happens to this stranger as they care about their own flesh and blood.

And this is exactly what we hear them do as Adam cries out, "This one at last is bone from my bones, flesh from my flesh." Eve and Adam overcome their "aloneness" and become fully human by recognizing and responding to the humanity of the stranger before them, by embracing the other as neighbor, companion, and friend. And in doing so they recognize and respond to the humanity of *every* stranger they will ever encounter—or be. They acknowledge that the flesh and blood of every foreigner, alien, and enemy is their flesh and blood. This completes the creation of the humans.

This moment of recognition and transformation parallels the creation of humans in Genesis 1:27, in which we read that humans are fashioned in the image and likeness of God and that God has made us in this image as male and female. That passage informs us that *all* persons are made in the divine image and that we are created in God's image as a community of different persons. In Genesis 2:23 the creation of humans is completed in the moment in which Eve and Adam recognize the other as fashioned in their own image and likeness, in the moment in which they see that the other is like me. In this moment the clay creatures become human by recognizing that the other or stranger—indeed *all* others and *all* strangers—are like me.

The moment in which Eve and Adam become human by recognizing and responding to each other's humanity is also a moment of great joy and aesthetic pleasure. In this moment the creatures becoming human beings experience something akin to God's pleasure at seeing the various stages (and totality) of creation. Indeed, we might say that Eve and Adam "saw that it was good" that "they were *not* alone" and saw with delight the goodness and beauty of this neighbor, who—like themselves—was fashioned in the image and likeness of God. In this moment of joyful recognition, Eve and Adam suddenly see the stranger before them as their beloved neighbor, friend, and companion. The "other" whom they thought was merely an "it" has become a "thou" who reaches out to them in joyous friendship.

This moment, shot through with beauty and joy, is the moment of seeing our child for the first time, of falling in love with our beloved, of seeing a familiar and friendly face in a strange place, of having our grown child come unexpectedly through the door. It is a moment of elation, awe, wonder, and beauty; for that which was foreign, strange, and threatening has been transformed into something friendly, familiar, and beloved. All our babies are beautiful. All our friends are a welcome sight. All our returning children are glorious to behold—because they are *ours* and we are *theirs*. And the beauty we see in their faces—in their shared humanity—renders us susceptible to love and care for them, to treat them justly.

The Ugly Stranger: An Inhuman Fiend

But we do not see the beauty of every human or the humanity of every stranger. Sometimes we see the other as a threat, inspiring fear and loathing. Sometimes we see the stranger as a creature we can use or abuse to our own advantage, a stepping stone to the "good life." In either case the "other" becomes an "it" instead of a "thou," and the stranger, instead of revealing herself as an undiscovered friend, morphs into an alien, enemy, or slave—a creature who is not of our flesh or bones and who can be abandoned, oppressed, or destroyed with abandon.

We balk at slaughtering, raping, or torturing our children or friends or neighbors because we see ourselves in them, because they are a part of us, because they are like us. And we resist oppressing or enslaving our fellow human beings because they are bone of our bones and flesh of our flesh. So in order to turn our beloved and our neighbors into enemies that we can maim, torture, and kill and aliens that we can abandon or enslave, we must "unsee" their beauty; we must forget our shared humanity and discover some markers that cut these strangers off from our shared flesh. We must unsee what Adam and Eve see in Genesis 2:23 and see instead an alien and monstrous flesh separate from the rest of us.

If we see beauty in the face of the neighbor and relative, if we see beauty when recognizing the shared humanity of the other who has become a "thou" to us, then what we see in the face of the alien who has become our enemy, victim, or slave must be ugliness. The stranger who frightens and threatens us, the opponent we are preparing to attack, defeat, or slaughter must appear to us as alien and strange. His flesh and bones must be transformed into foreign and threatening territory. He must be rendered ugly and monstrous—or the sight of his or her shared humanity would sap our terror and rage, stripping us of the ability to maim, torture, and kill. And the alien whose oppression and enslavement offers us such advantages cannot be recognized as our sibling or child, lest we surrender our power, prestige, or wealth. We must cover over the humanity of these enemies and aliens we would kill and enslave with a monstrous ugliness that masks our shared humanity. For this monstrous ugliness evokes rage and disgust, reminding us that "it" could not possibly be bone from our bones, flesh from our flesh.

Rendering the Stranger Ugly: Three Paths

In the musical *South Pacific* Oscar Hammerstein tells us:

You've got to be taught to be afraid,
Of people whose eyes are oddly made,
And people whose skin is a different shade,
You've got to be carefully taught.[2]

Adam's cry in Genesis 2:23 reminds us that *every* stranger is our flesh and blood, that every other is like us, and that we can see this *imago hominis* in every human face. To ignore and overlook this shared humanity—staring us right in the face, so to speak—we need to be carefully taught to unsee the neighbor and sibling standing before us and transform this friend into an alien, stranger, or enemy. To alienate ourselves from this self-evident neighbor, from this obvious sibling, to prepare ourselves to ignore the moral ties binding us to these fellow humans, to get ready to abandon, enslave, torture, or slaughter this bone of our bone and flesh of our flesh, we must be taught to unmake these human beings and recreate them as beasts and fiends who are not like us.

To bring about this alienation, we must learn to unsee the shared history, culture, language, and humanity of neighboring tribes, communities, or nations and to focus on and magnify out of proportion the real and imagined differences between ourselves and these people. To help us unsee our ties to these unrecognized neighbors, the alien who is to become an enemy must be disfigured and made ugly. The flesh of these strangers must incorporate the threat we believe they pose and must be turned into something foreign and monstrous—into something that is distinctly *not like us*.[3]

And so the aesthetic transformation of the enemy into a monstrous beast is an essential part of the propaganda machinery of alienation, oppression, and war. Abandonment, enslavement, hate, torture, and slaughter require tremendous energy since they must overcome any natural sympathy for the strangers we seek to destroy and can only be sustained as long as we forget or mask the shared humanity tying us to these creatures.

Truth, the ancient Greek dramatist Aeschylus wrote, is the first casualty of war. And the first truth war annihilates is the shared humanity that binds us to our foes. For before we can wage war, injuring and destroying the

[2] Oscar Hammerstein II, "You've Got to Be Carefully Taught," from *South Pacific*, by Richard Rogers and Oscar Hammerstein II, 1949.

[3] Anthony Synnott, "Truth and Goodness, Mirrors and Masks Part II: A Sociology of Beauty and the Face," *The British Journal of Sociology* 41, no. 1 (March 1990): 56.

bodies of thousands or millions of our enemies, we must first blind ourselves to the truth that these bodies are bone of our bones and flesh of our flesh. We must turn the flesh of neighbors into something foreign and monstrous.

War is hard enough when we are forced to look upon and mourn the destroyed beauty of the sons and daughters we have sacrificed in battle, when we must grieve our own nation's dead and wounded children. But war becomes impossible if we must also recognize dead and wounded enemies as bone of our bone and flesh of our flesh, if we must mourn and grieve the maiming and slaughter of our enemies' children as if they were our own. That would be too much to bear. To tolerate the murderous ugliness of war, we must at least teach ourselves not to see the humanity of the wounded and dying bodies of our foes.

In a similar fashion, slavery demands that we teach ourselves not to see the humanity of those neighbors placed in chains. For slavery and every form of racism, discrimination, and oppression demands that we ignore or overlook the humanity of those we marginalize, abuse, and enslave. We must teach ourselves to stifle any natural sympathy or compassion for these strangers whom we violate and oppress. To tolerate the massive violence and suffering inflicted upon those we subjugate, imprison, or persecute, we must transform the flesh of our neighbor into something strange, monstrous, and inferior. We could not stand ourselves if we were behaving so fiendishly to the bone of our bones and the flesh of our flesh.

The "uglification" of the stranger—transforming them into monstrous enemies or aliens who are not like us—takes place in at least three different ways:

1. *Distorting the image.* The first approach is to caricature or demonize these unrecognized neighbors as monsters, vermin, fiends, insects, and so on. This is done through propaganda, satire, ridicule, and so forth.

2. *Degrading the environment.* A second approach is to degrade the habitat, environment, clothing, and appearance of our neighbors, placing them in a context of filth and squalor that dehumanizes them in our eyes. We immerse them in and smudge them with squalor, transforming them into waste and rubbish.

3. *Disfiguring the person.* The final approach is to mark or disfigure the persons being prepared for destruction. The attack on their habitat

now moves to their flesh; abusing, assaulting, branding, maiming, raping, and torturing the bodies of our neighbors in an attempt to degrade and disfigure the humanity staring back at us transforms them into something we no longer recognize as flesh of our flesh.

DISTORTING THE IMAGE

Umberto Eco argues there has long been a tendency to portray strangers and enemies as ugly and demonic beasts. The ancient Greeks and Romans cast their foes as pug-nosed and unkempt barbarians, while Christianity painted Jews, Saracens, and heretics as vile, foul, and brutish creatures. In the political caricatures of more recent times, religious and national enemies were drawn with "grotesque or wicked-looking features" and described as monstrous beasts. [4]

In *Faces of the Enemy* Sam Keen shows over and over again how the wartime propaganda machinery of modern states transforms the leaders and citizens of enemy nations into monstrous and despicable beasts who may be slaughtered without remorse.[5] In hundreds of posters and cartoons the rulers and people of Germany, Japan, Russia, England, France, and the United States are made over in the image and likeness of sadistic and godless villains, criminals, torturers, and rapists, as well as reptiles, vermin, and insects. As Keen's book illustrates, citizens are prepared for war and anesthetized to its horrific violence by propaganda campaigns that transfigure the bodies of our opponents into grotesque barbarians, frightening demons, and ghoulish fiends whose monstrous flesh is fashioned of something foreign and strange—something not like us. To justify and tolerate wars that turn thousands or millions of human bodies into corpses and that maim and scar millions or tens of millions of other bodies, we must first transform these bodies in our imagination into something monstrous and inhuman.

Jeffrey Herf argues in *The Jewish Enemy* that massive propaganda campaigns caricaturing and demonizing Jews as money-hungry villains, sexual perverts, and filthy vermin were an essential part of the Nazi plan for the Holocaust.[6] In the early to late 1930s, Nazi leaders relied upon

---

[4] Umberto Eco, *On Ugliness* (London: Rizzoli, 2007), 185–97.

[5] Sam Keen, *Faces of the Enemy: Reflections of the Hostile Imagination* (San Francisco: Harper and Row, 1986).

[6] Jeffrey Herf, *The Jewish Enemy: Nazi Propaganda during World War II and the Holocaust* (Cambridge, MA: Belknap Press, 2006).

long-standing European and German anti-Semitism to pass laws that stripped German Jews of property, status, and legal rights, increasingly marginalizing them from German society. But in order to justify the horrific "final solution" of the Holocaust, Hitler had Nazi propagandists like Joseph Goebbels and Otto Dietrich launch a "ubiquitous and intrusive" media campaign vilifying Jews as enemies of the state and dehumanizing them as vermin.[7] The goal of this campaign, which permeated every aspect of the ordinary German's life, was to provoke rage and hatred against Jews and to justify a monstrous and unimaginable crime.

A cornerstone of this pervasive, intrusive, and accelerated campaign of hate was the Ministry for Public Enlightenment and Propaganda *Word of the Week* wall newspaper, a highly graphic weekly displayed in tens and sometimes hundreds of thousands of public places throughout Germany and Austria. Hardly any strolling, commuting, or laboring citizen could avoid these political posters designed as newspapers or miss the visual propaganda portraying Jews as dangerous criminals and villainous beasts.[8] Images of Jews as greedy and rapacious financiers or villainous and beastly conspirators were displayed in every factory, marketplace, train station, bus stop, butcher shop, bank office, and government building. Dehumanizing political cartoons portrayed Jews as serpents, demons, or apes, and Jewish characters were given huge hooked noses, unkempt beards, and claws.[9] To justify the planned horror of the Holocaust, it was necessary to turn Jews into alien monsters who could be exterminated as fiends.

One of the great ironies of the Nazi propaganda campaign, which served up hundreds of thousands of caricatures and cartoons of Jews with distorted and grotesque features, was that the Nazi officials could not, in fact, distinguish Jewish citizens from their neighbors based on appearance alone. This, Herf notes, is the reason the Nazi regime demanded that Jews wear the yellow Star of David, lest they pass as ordinary citizens—which is what they looked like.[10] The propaganda machine that transformed Jews into vermin and beasts was, from start to finish, a lie; and the Nazis had to institute identity cards and badges

---

[7] Ibid., 14.

[8] Ibid., 28–36.

[9] Alexander Alvarez, "Adjusting to Genocide: The Techniques of Neutralization and the Holocaust," *Social Science History* 21, no. 2 (Summer 1997): 166–67.

[10] Herf, *The Jewish Enemy*, 151.

because these Jewish neighbors looked just like every other German, Austrian, and Pole.

Half a century after the Holocaust, the Hutu government of Rwanda and its supporters carried out an escalating campaign of racial hatred, violence, and genocide against the Tutsi minority of that nation. This time wall newspapers were replaced by talk radio stations spewing all sorts of vitriol and calumny against an ethnic minority being scapegoated for a host of social and economic problems caused largely by inept, corrupt, and greedy leaders. Africa scholars Peter Uvin and Helen Hintjens both argue that the genocide in Rwanda was made possible by a systematic campaign of propaganda meant to fuel paranoid and racist hatred against the Tutsi.[11]

In the widespread propaganda campaign leading up to the genocide committed in April and May of 1994, Tutsi were "constantly the subject of the most hateful propaganda."[12] In political rallies and speeches, in the columns of native papers, and on the airwaves of Radio Libre des Miles Collines, Tutsi were vilified as demons and monsters and described as "cockroaches" that needed to be exterminated.

Here too, however, the hate campaign collapsed in irony. For though racist propaganda asserted over and over that Tutsis were strikingly different in appearance from the majority Hutus, a number of leading social scientists report that "the Rwandans are basically a single ethnic group, with differences between Hutu and Tutsi reflecting socio-economic divisions," and Hintjens notes that the vast majority of those slaughtered in the 1994 Rwandan genocide "were small rural Tutsi who were in no way different from their Hutu neighbors."[13] In fact, many Hutus were mistakenly killed during the genocide because they were thought to look like Tutsis.

The truth is that it is quite impossible to tell the difference between the Hutus and Tutsis pictured in *Intimate Enemy: Images and Voices of the Rwandan Genocide*, Scott Straus and Robert Lyons's book of photographs of genocide perpetrators and survivors.[14] This may explain why both

---

[11] Peter Uvin, "Prejudice, Crisis, and Genocide in Rwanda," *African Studies Review* 40, no. 2 (September 1997): 91–115. Helen Hintjens, "Explaining the 1994 Genocide in Rwanda," *The Journal of Modern African Studies* 37, no. 2 (1990): 241–86.

[12] Uvin, "Prejudice, Crisis, and Genocide in Rwanda," 110.

[13] Ibid., 93; Hintjens, "Explaining the 1994 Genocide in Rwanda," 247.

[14] Scott Straus and Robert Lyons, *Intimate Enemy: Images and Voices of the Rwandan Genocide* (Brooklyn, NY: Zone Books, 2006).

the colonial and the subsequent Hutu government had long employed ethnic identity cards to tell members of the two tribes apart and to reinforce the myth of separate ethnic identity. For even as the 1994 hate campaign was leading hundreds of thousands of Hutus to the brink of genocide, most of these people could not tell the difference between themselves and their Tutsi neighbors. The campaign of racial hatred (meant to distract Hutus from larger social and political ills) relied on segregation laws, identity cards, and racial myths to create a sense of difference where one hardly existed. The people being slaughtered looked just like the people doing the slaughtering—as if they were bone of the same bone and flesh of the same flesh.

Justifying the enslavement of tens of millions of Africans also required white Europeans and Americans to blind themselves to the shared humanity and beauty of the legions of neighbors they kidnapped, oppressed, tortured, and murdered. At first the biblical legend of Ham was used to show that Africans, who were supposedly Ham's descendants, were a cursed race, fit only for a life of bondage. But later leading Enlightenment thinkers like Immanuel Kant, Carl Linnaeus, and Georg Wilhelm Friedrich Hegel articulated a pseudoscientific racist theory that presented Africans as a separate, inferior, and not fully human race of people who lacked the intelligence, virtue, and beauty of Caucasians.[15]

Adopting a classical Greek aesthetic, Enlightenment critics like J. J.Winkleman (who never visited Greece) and Johann Friedrich Blumenbach argued that Europeans and Caucasians were the only truly beautiful humans, while Kant, Linnaeus, and David Hume divided humanity into four or five separate and profoundly unequal species, with Africans at the bottom of the scale. Hegel contended that the African was "nothing more than a savage" and urged his readers to think not "of a spiritual God or of moral laws" when considering this beast.[16] Over and over, Enlightenment texts described Africans as inferior, immoral, and ugly. The enslavement and brutalization of millions of these strangers could be justified because they did not look like us and because they were not bone of our bone and flesh of our flesh.

In 1850 Louis Agassiz, the founding director of Harvard's museum of comparative zoology and probably the most famous scientist in America at that point, set out to establish the separate and inferior status of the

---

[15] James Logan, *Good Punishment? Christian Moral Practice and U.S. Imprisonment* (Grand Rapids, MI: Eerdmans, 2008), 115–26.

[16] Ibid., 119–23.

African race by commissioning a series of daguerreotypes of male and female slaves on a North Carolina plantation.[17] Agassiz, a proslavery advocate with strong racist feelings, had become convinced (from a single encounter with black servants in a boarding house) that Africans "are not of the same blood as us," and he hoped the daguerreotypes of naked and seminaked slaves would show that European whites were a superior race and that African blacks were the product of a separate creation.[18]

Brian Wallis writes in "Black Bodies, White Science" that Agassiz was part of a larger "scientific" movement seeking to justify slavery by establishing the separate genesis of the races and showing the moral and physical inferiority of Africans.[19] At the same time, the daguerreotypes Agassiz commissioned fit into a larger pattern of so-called scientific photographs of blacks, showing them with abnormally pronounced features, undressed, or clad in torn rags, as well as beaten, branded, or whipped—all in the hope of communicating a message that Africans were an inferior race fit only for subjugation by whites.[20] Like Nazi cartoons of "invidious" Jews, these "scientific" photographs were meant to teach viewers to unsee the beauty and humanity of Africans kidnapped into slavery.

James Samuel Logan argues that even after slavery had ended, white America needed a justification for the racism and injustice of segregation and for the massive and disproportionate incarceration of millions of African American males.[21] In the decades after the Civil War, slavery was replaced by Jim Crow laws that alienated, marginalized, and oppressed millions of ex-slaves, and the South's already racist prison system was increasingly transformed into a black penal colony where black males were imprisoned and put to work as slave laborers.[22]

Justifying the massive and disproportionate incarceration of black males, which has only increased and become more and more widespread in the past 150 years, demanded that African American men be vilified as horrible beasts and monsters who could not control themselves and

---

[17] Mary Warner Marien, *Photography: A Cultural History* (New York: Harry N. Abrams, 2002), 40–41; Brian Wallis, "Black Bodies, White Science: Louis Agassiz's Slave Daguerreotypes," *Art in America* 9, no. 2 (Summer 1995): 40.

[18] Wallis, "Black Bodies, White Science," 42–43.

[19] Ibid., 42–46.

[20] Ibid., 52–54.

[21] Logan, *Good Punishment?*, 126–41.

[22] Ibid., 138.

who posed a terrible threat to society.[23] And as the percentage of prisoners who are black males has grown and grown over the decades, so has the tendency to treat these prisoners as incorrigible beasts and to describe them as "filth," "dirt," "slime," "scum," "excrement," "pieces of shit," "diseased," "contagious," "wreckage," "debris," and "monsters."[24] Tolerating a prison system that incarcerates young black males at such an alarming and disproportionate rate demands that the larger society be carefully taught not to see the humanity or beauty of these young men.

DEGRADING THE ENVIRONMENT

If we are going to abandon, oppress, or destroy our neighbors, it is not enough to distort their image into something ugly; we must also render their habitat ugly and mean, staining them with the smudge of filth and squalor. Christopher Gestrich argues that "people who are headed for destruction are first deprived of their honor, stripped of their rights, and their outward performance takes on a pathetic, ugly form."[25]

John Steinbeck tracks this process of degradation and destruction in his classic novel *The Grapes of Wrath*. Early on, a ghostly and broken Muley Graves whines that he and his neighbors have been destroyed by the bankers who stripped them of their modest homes and hardscrabble farms, driving them onto the open road and crowding them into filthy and unsanitary squatters' camps and "Hoovervilles," where they live and are treated like animals. "Place where folks live is them folks," Muley complains. "They ain't whole, out lonely on the road in a piled up car. They ain't alive no more. The sons-a-bitches killed 'em."[26] And in the course of Steinbeck's novel, legions of homeless farmers like the Joads are stripped of their pride and dignity and transformed into bitter and frightened refugees, despised and abused by employers, and hunted by police and health inspectors who treat them as unwanted and dangerous vermin.[27]

Most species are driven into extinction by the degradation and destruction of their habitat. And when we are preparing to abandon or destroy

---

[23] Ibid., 139.

[24] Ibid., 25.

[25] Christoph Gestrich, *The Return of Splendor in the World* (Grand Rapids, MI: Eerdmans, 1997), 1.

[26] John Steinbeck, *The Grapes of Wrath* (New York: Penguin, 2002), 52.

[27] Ibid., 237.

other humans, it helps to degrade and destroy their environment as well. For the places where we work and live can nurture and support us, providing us with a modicum of health, safety, and sustenance and expressing and celebrating our humanity, creativity, and dignity. Or they can threaten, alienate, and overwhelm us, sapping our physical and emotional health, stripping us of opportunity, safety, and a sense of self-worth, and driving us to despair, crime, and violence.

Timothy Gorringe argues that the architecture of our built environment is a "third skin" we inhabit, and that the homes and cities we live in express and reflect our society's underlying sense of theology and justice.[28] From our palatial cathedrals to our crime-ridden slums, from our glistening skyscrapers to our squalid refugee camps, and from our gated communities to our maximum-security prisons, our buildings, infrastructure, and architecture make moral and political statements, telling us who is more or less important or human and how different classes and races of persons should be treated. The world we make with brick and mortar makes a moral and political statement about who we are and about who counts as human. And because we live and breathe in this architecture all the time—because it is before us, beneath us, and behind us—these lessons sink deep into our unconscious and shape how we see and imagine the world and our neighbors.[29]

So if we are going to teach ourselves to unsee the humanity and beauty of strangers, we need to place them in degraded buildings, cities, and environments so that we can mask the humanity they share with us. By housing strangers and aliens in horrid, overcrowded, filthy, and barren places, we teach ourselves (and them) to see them as less than human. The function, then, of slums, barrios, and ghettos—or squatter, refugee and concentration camps—is not merely to place these others in a separate place, but to put them in separate *and* unequal places, degraded and dehumanized places that reinforce the notion that these strangers are not like us and so can be abandoned, oppressed, or destroyed as necessary.

Millions of Africans snared in the Atlantic slave trade were first shackled like chattel and then crammed by the hundreds into overcrowded holds, mid-decks, and steerage of slave ships, where they lay packed next to one another on bare wooden shelves like so many cuts of beef.

---

[28] Tim Gorringe, *A Theology of the Built Environment* (New York: Cambridge University Press, 2002), 7.

[29] Ibid., 82.

In short order these crowded quarters turned foul, filthy, disgusting, and dangerous, and large numbers of kidnapped Africans grew sick and died from a range of fevers and diseases or took their lives in despair.[30]

When sold into slavery in America, the Africans and their descendents were first housed in barns and barracks, then moved into slave cabins that were "cramped, crudely built, scantily furnished, unpainted, and dirty."[31] Most of these cabins were "little different from the outbuildings where slaveholders housed their animals and stored their tools."[32] Bare, filthy, and crowded, these cabins came with leaky roofs, open floors, and mud fireplaces that often caught fire. And they were widely recognized as "laboratories of disease," believed to be the largest single cause of sickness and death among African American slaves.[33]

It can be argued that captured Africans and their descendents were crammed into foul and degrading quarters on slave ships and plantations to save their captors and slaveholders money. But these filthy and dehumanizing environments were also chosen to send a message: that these strangers were not fully human creatures, that men and women living in such filth and muck were more like animals stabled in a pen than humans living in homes. The fact that so many slaveholders continued to house their workers in unsafe and unsanitary quarters even though they knew that these disease-infested cabins cost them significant amounts of money and labor suggests that they were motivated by more than economic concerns. Slaveholders wanted and needed to degrade and dehumanize the neighbors they had enslaved, and they did this by housing them in places that were ugly, filthy, and foul.

In the century after the Civil War, the descendents of emancipated slaves found that segregation and Jim Crow laws continued to press them into places that were separate and unequal. African Americans were relegated to inferior and dilapidated schools, neighborhoods, and housing, excluded from good stores, restaurants, theaters, and churches, and forced to ride in the backs of buses and trains. In both the South and North, Africans were segregated into poor neighborhoods and crowded

---

[30] Daniel P. Mannix, *Black Cargoes: A History of the Atlantic Slave Trade 1518–1865* (New York: Viking Press, 1962), 107–23.

[31] Kenneth M. Stamp, *The Peculiar Institution: Slavery in the Ante-Bellum South* (New York: Alfred A. Knopf, 1956), 294.

[32] Ira Berlin, *Many Thousands Gone: The First Two Centuries of Slavery in North America* (Cambridge, MA: Belknap Press, 1998), 131.

[33] Stamp, *The Peculiar Institution*, 295.

into ghettos and slums. And a grossly disproportionate number of African Americans were squeezed into the nation's burgeoning jails and prisons.

And, as we saw earlier, recent studies show that the communities where African Americans and other minorities live and work are also the places where our society dumps disproportionately large amounts of its toxic waste, garbage, and pollution. Communities of color are more likely to be chosen as the location for toxic waste sites, hazardous waste landfills, garbage dumps, and incinerators.[34] And because they get much less help safeguarding them from the effects of all this waste or cleaning up these poisons, minority communities suffer from much more environmental pollution and degradation.

Crowding people into separate and unequal places, overcrowded and exhausted places that are ridden with crime, filth, and disease, serves to taint or smudge these strangers with the squalor of their degraded and dehumanized environment. Polluting their communities with toxic waste and foul garbage serves to contaminate these neighbors with ugliness. And it helps the rest of us to forget that these people are just like us.

Dehumanizing others by degrading their habitat and immersing them in filth and squalor was also a critical part of the Nazi process of the Holocaust. Preparing the German people to acquiesce to and participate in the extermination policies of the Nazis required a process of dehumanization by which the Jewish people were transformed into nonpersons who could be abandoned and destroyed.[35]

Along with other processes, this dehumanization involved stripping Jews of their political and civil rights, barring them from professions,

---

[34] Vernice D. Miller, "Building on Our Past, Planning for Our Future," in *Toxic Struggles: The Theory and Practice of Environmental Justice*, ed. Richard Hofrichter (Philadelphia, PA: New Society Publishers, 1993), 128; Robert D. Bullard, "Anatomy of Environmental Racism and the Environmental Justice Movement," in *Confronting Environmental Racism: Voices from the Grassroots*, ed. Robert D. Bullard (Boston, MA: South End Press, 1993), 19; Aaron Sachs, *Eco-Justice: Linking Human Rights and the Environment*, Worldwatch Paper 127 (Washington, DC: Worldwatch Institute, 1995), 10; Benjamin Goldman and Laura Fitton, *Toxic Wastes and Race Revisited: An Update of the 1987 Report on the Racial and Socioeconomic Characteristics of Communities with Hazardous Waste Sites* (Washington, DC: Center for Policy Alternatives, 1994), executive summary.

[35] Ronald J. Berger, "The 'Banality of Evil' Reframed: The Social Construction of the 'Final Solution' to the 'Jewish Problem,'" *The Sociological Quarterly* 34, no. 4 (November 1993): 611–12; Alvarez, "Adjusting to Genocide," 166–68.

and taking away their businesses and property. But it was also necessary to remake the Jewish people in the image and likeness of the vile caricatures of Nazi propaganda, to transform them into the subhuman vermin the Nazis imagined them to be. And this dehumanization required that Jews be forced from the homes and neighborhoods that supported and nurtured them and herded like cattle or cargo into ghettos and concentration camps where, with "heads shaved, covered in their own waste, and emaciated beyond recognition," these inmates "were hardly recognizable as human beings." [36]

By stripping Jews of their clothing and jewelry, immersing them in crowded, filthy, and unsanitary quarters, and working and starving them into an emaciated state, "the Germans succeeded in making many of the camp system's inhabitants take on the appearance—including festering, open wounds, and the marks of disease and illness—and behavioral attributes of the 'subhumans' that the Germans imagined them to be." [37] When the commandant of Treblinka was asked why it was necessary to degrade and dehumanize people who were being prepared for destruction, he responded, "To condition those who actually had to carry out the policies—to make it possible for them to do what they did." [38] Inmates in the camps were kept in appalling circumstances, "systematically subjected to filth," and made "the deliberate target of excremental assault" so that these foul nonpersons would be seen as "not human like us," and so their murderers could sleep with an undisturbed conscience. [39]

DISFIGURING THE PERSON

Transforming our neighbors into ugly and unrecognizable strangers culminates with an assault on their flesh. Caricaturing them as vermin and immersing them in filth prepares us to inflict this final injury. It is easier to abuse and attack those we have refashioned as fiends and penned as beasts. But the assault on our unrecognized neighbor's flesh is also a part of making them ugly. We do not rape, torture, maim, beat, whip, brand, or scar merely to inflict pain, but also—even primarily—to put a mark on our victims that will identify them as subhuman. We may

---

[36] Alvarez, "Adjusting to Genocide," 168.

[37] Daniel Jonah Goldhagen, *Hitler's Willing Executioners: Ordinary Germans and the Holocaust* (New York: Knopf, 1996), 176.

[38] Alvarez, "Adjusting to Genocide," 168.

[39] Ibid.

have to prepare ourselves for this attack by demonizing our neighbors and covering them with slime, but the assault itself is an attempt to transform our fellow human beings into ugly beasts. Adam recognizes the humanity of Eve when he looks upon her flesh and bones and recognizes these bones and flesh as his own. The violence we inflict on others is an attempt to render their flesh and bones unrecognizable as human.

The practice of slavery required not only that Africans be caricatured and quartered as beasts but also that their bodies be marked and scarred as slaves, so that no one would forget that these people were but chattel and property. Slave traders, overseers, and owners routinely beat, whipped, scourged, and branded their captives and slaves, scarring, burning, and laying open the wounded flesh of Africans who forgot that they were beasts or refused to accept their bondage as chattel. The brand and whip were meant to "teach a lesson" by inscribing the beastliness of these slaves into their very flesh. In nineteenth-century pictures of African slaves, "the body itself was often shown being whipped, beaten, hung, pierced, bitten, branded, or otherwise subjugated to a white oppressor." [40] These, the publishers of such images seemed to argue, were the bodies not of free and noble human beings but of beasts.

And during and after Reconstruction, thousands of African Americans were whipped, tortured, and lynched—often before white mobs that were entertained and assured by the sight of scarred and murdered African bodies. Postcard images of these tortured and lynched bodies sold well throughout the South, reinforcing the white supremacist argument that African Americans were not fully human and needed to be kept in their place. Exhibiting the image of these tortured and destroyed bodies was meant to teach a lesson: such slaughtered creatures are not like us.

Rape is an assault on the body intended to degrade and dehumanize the abused and violated neighbor. The rapist seeks to subjugate his victim, to establish his dominion over the neighbor he treats as a beast. In this act of sadistic abuse rapists attempt to degrade their victims, marking them out as subhuman creatures. The wartime rape of women is an attempt to disgrace and destroy a people by dehumanizing women in a sadistic and beastly fashion, turning mothers and sisters and daughters into whores, and tainting and staining them with the mark of this horrible

---

[40] Wallis, "Black Bodies, White Science," 53.

crime. The rape of captives and slaves is meant to reinforce their sub-human status by treating them as mindless and powerless puppets and branding and defiling them as so much meat. And the rape of prisoners and inmates is an essential part of their ongoing degradation and dehu-manization, of their being marked out as subhuman beasts beyond the pale of our concern or compassion.[41]

Torture, too, is meant to teach a lesson about the inhumanity of those who are subjected to this violence. In the practice of torture a sharp line is drawn between those who torture and those who get tortured. Before they can inflict their sadistic abuse, torturers must convince themselves that their victims are not like us, that the bodies they beat, electrocute, and scourge are not fully human. But the torture itself is a part of this dehumanizing and degrading process. Indeed, it is its culmination. For in this horrendous assault the torturer seeks to transform the bodies of his neighbors into something vile, subhuman, and disgusting. With the bestial instruments of torture he inscribes his belief in the inhumanity of his victims into the very flesh of those he beats, and he forces that broken flesh to cry out, confessing its inferiority. With this torture the abuser seeks to erase or disappear the humanity of his victims.

As Elaine Scarry argues in *The Body in Pain*, torture first strips victims of their safe, familiar, and nurturing environs by immersing them in a foreign, dangerous, and terrifying world in which they are subject to the endless threat of unbearable and escalating pain.[42] Then, by means of this threat and pain, the victims' own bodies are transformed into a dangerous and frightening beast that overwhelms and annihilates them. The hostility and disdain the torturer bears toward the bodies he beats and shocks is internalized by his tortured victims, whose flesh and bones have become a conduit of the torturer's rage and cruelty. For the victims of torture, their own bodies have betrayed them and become a monstrous threat. They are shattered and ravaged by flesh and bones that are no longer theirs, by bodies that have turned ugly and cruel. And for the torturer, the haunted faces, broken sobs, and ruined flesh of his victims confirm his belief in their inhumanity.

Ancient Rome tortured its enemies publicly, terrorizing subjugated peoples by crucifying thousands of rebels, subversives, and slaves who

---

[41] Logan, *Good Punishment?*, 35.

[42] Elaine Scarry, *The Body in Pain: The Making and Unmaking of the World* (New York: Oxford University Press: 1987), 27–60.

dared to assert their liberty or equality.[43] In Palestine and elsewhere, Rome reacted to revolts with mass crucifixions, lining the roads and public squares with the shattered and broken bodies of its foes, forcing every passerby to look on these dying and rotting bodies and remember the folly of thinking that creatures such as these were equal to Rome or its citizens.

And the public lesson of torture did not end with death, for the corpses of the crucified were left on their beams and crosses to rot or be devoured by vultures and packs of feral dogs. This final and degrading destruction of the bodies of the tortured was meant to drive home the lesson that these unburied, rotting corpses were not human. They were merely the decaying meat and bones of beasts.

Modern states prefer to torture in private and are reticent to parade the results of their barbarity before the public. So the victims of torture are not held up as a public lesson but tend to be disappeared by the government that has abused and violated them. Sometimes they are dropped into the ocean. Other times they are dumped in open and shallow graves. In either case, the lesson is the same. Bodies that have been rendered ugly by the abuse and violence of torture are now further degraded by being deprived of the burial and mourning accorded every human being. After having their flesh violated and shattered, the tortured and exterminated are transformed into dirt without any grief or ceremony, without any human recognition that here was a person like any one of us.

In the Holocaust as well, the process of rendering the neighbor ugly culminated in degrading and dehumanizing assaults on the body, including torture, murder, and disposal. After being vilified as vermin and immersed in filth, Jews had their heads shaved and their arms tattooed. Then they were subjected to a reign of terror, torture, forced labor, starvation, and filth that turned their bodies into stumbling corpses and covered their flesh with festering wounds and infections.[44] Nearly unrecognizable as humans, these dead women and men walking were then herded into gas chambers, exterminated like beasts, and disposed of like cargo.

Like disappeared torture victims, the annihilation of Holocaust victims was not complete until every trace of their humanity had been erased.

[43] William R. Herzog, *Prophet and Teacher: An Introduction to the Historical Jesus* (Louisville, KY: Westminster John Knox Press, 2005), 227–29.
[44] Berger, "The 'Banality of Evil' Reframed," 612.

So in the concentration and death camps, the bodies of the murdered were not to be recognized as human remains to be mourned, buried, or treated with respect. As two camp survivors later wrote, "The Germans even forbade us to use the word 'corpse' or 'victim.' The dead were blocks of wood, shit, with absolutely no importance. Anyone who said 'corpse' or 'victim' was beaten. The Germans made us refer to the bodies as Figuren, that is, as puppets, as dolls, or as Schmattes, which means 'rags.' "[45] At every stage the humanity of the neighbor who is being abandoned, oppressed, and destroyed must be hidden from view. This "block of wood" is not bone of my bone or flesh of my flesh.

WOMEN AND BEAUTY: A SPECIAL CASE

We render strangers and enemies ugly because the grotesque and monstrous inspires fear and loathing. The humans we remake in the image and likeness of monsters and beasts do not evoke compassion or concern but apathy and hostility, enabling us to abandon, abuse, and destroy these unrecognized neighbors with an undisturbed conscience. We have made them ugly and may now do with them what we will.

But beauty can also frighten us, and the fear of beauty's power to move us or to render us vulnerable can provoke hostility toward those who are beautiful. In patriarchal and sexist societies women are endlessly praised and extolled for their beauty. But they are also marginalized, oppressed, and violated—to no small degree because they are beautiful and because the power of their beauty frightens men.

There are, of course, plenty of women among the strangers, enemies, and slaves rendered ugly to justify their abuse and destruction. Caricatures and propaganda degrading slaves and Holocaust victims ridiculed and parodied women as well. Half the people crammed into the filth and squalor of slave ships and quarters or herded into ghettos and camps were women. And women have swelled the ranks of the victims of degrading and dehumanizing violence, making up the overwhelming majority of rape's victims.

But women have also been marginalized, oppressed, abused, and destroyed because of their beauty. For the feminine beauty so highly praised and demanded in patriarchal societies is also the object of considerable fear and suspicion. The ubiquitous male gaze that expects and

<hr>

[45] Alvarez, "Adjusting to Genocide," 161.

seeks out female beauty is intimidated by and suspicious of this beauty's power. Such intoxicating and seductive beauty, the argument goes, cannot be fully human. In the patriarchal mindset, women's physical beauty ties them to the lower order of the natural world or tags them as demonic temptresses who threaten to seduce and corrupt manly virtue.[46] In either case, instead of identifying women as neighbors, partners, and friends, their beauty is often transformed into a badge that marks them out as strange, dangerous, and subhuman. In this way female beauty becomes, ironically enough, a justification for the marginalization, abuse, and destruction of women.

The beauty of women is turned against them and used to justify their dehumanization in a number of ways. As already mentioned, this beauty is often seen as linking them with sinful desires and temptations. Leading Christian authors like Tertullian, Augustine, and Jerome warned of the seductive or demonic power of female beauty and chastised women who sought to enhance this beauty for being temptresses and whores. Modest or virtuous Christian women were encouraged to hide or disfigure their beauty to render themselves less threatening and more holy.[47]

At the same time, female beauty becomes a justification for the objectification, oppression, and abuse of women. Contemporary advertizing sells every manner of product by draping a half-naked woman over or around the merchandize in question. Millions of women around the planet are kidnapped and trafficked as sex workers and slaves in a degrading and dehumanizing industry intent on pleasing male sexual appetites. And rapists continue to blame their victims for dressing and behaving too seductively and provocatively.

Meanwhile, millions of women in Islamic societies are forced to hide their bodies and are barred from getting an education, participating in politics, or even learning to drive at least in part because their beauty threatens and intimidates those in power in these patriarchal nations.

As Naomi Wolf has pointed out, beauty is also used as a trap to oppress and marginalize women. In societies where the male gaze is always hungry for and seeking out female beauty, women are repeatedly told

[46] Susan Ross, "Women, Beauty, and Justice: Moving beyond von Balthasar," *Journal of the Society of Christian Ethics* 25, no. 1 (2005): 80.

[47] Ibid. See also Susan Ross, *For the Beauty of the Earth: Women, Sacramentality, and Justice* (New York: Paulist Press, 2006), 16–21.

they are not beautiful enough.[48] The female body is under constant scrutiny and subject to endless and unfavorable comparisons. Women are reminded over and over that they are not (ever) beautiful enough. And in pursuit of this elusive beauty they are pressed to spend disproportionate money and time and even to risk and harm themselves and their health. In this way women are made foreigners to their own bodies and distracted from their own development and fair participation in the larger society. From the time they are small girls, women are told they are ugly creatures who must wage a constant war on their own flesh in order to meet the expectations of the patriarchal stare.

Finally, it seems a curious irony that the very patriarchal societies that prize and extol female beauty tend to assign the most filthy and degrading jobs to women. In her essay "Dirt and Economic Inequality," Christine Firer Hinze notes the concentration of women in "dirty" jobs where workers tend to the mess and detritus of human bodies.[49] The people who have to do the ugly, degrading, and filthy work of cleaning up our waste, clearing our plates, washing our linens, changing our sheets and diapers, cleaning our underwear, mopping up our excrement and feces, and tending our wounds, infections, and ulcers are mostly women. And these jobs, unlike dirty jobs in construction or waste management, are consistently undervalued and underpaid positions of low status. So the intimidating beauty of women is blotted out by immersing them in the muck of human waste.

Recognizing the Beauty of the Stranger: Biblical Voices

The Hebrew Bible

More than a few biblical passages attack and demonize strangers, aliens, and enemies, calling for or accepting their oppression, abuse, or even annihilation. The enemies of Israel are often cursed, condemned, and sentenced to execution, while those strangers and foreigners who inhabit the land promised to the Hebrews are to be conquered, expelled, or exterminated. In several places in Scripture the stranger is not recog-

---

[48] Naomi Wolf, *The Beauty Myth: How Images of Beauty Are Used against Women* (New York: HarperCollins, 2002). See also Ross, *For the Beauty of the Earth*, 14–16; Sheila Jeffries, *Beauty and Misogyny: Harmful Cultural Practices in the West* (New York: Routledge, 2005).

[49] Christine Firer Hinze, "Dirt and Economic Inequality: A Christian-Ethical Peek under the Rug," *Annual of the Society of Christian Ethics* 21 (2001): 45–62.

nized as fully human, as flesh of our flesh and bone of our bone. And a number of the passages cursing and calling for the destruction of strangers and enemies have been used to justify abuse and violence inflicted on opponents and enemies.

Still, there is a chorus of biblical voices proclaiming and defending the beauty and humanity of the stranger, summoning us to recognize that the alien and enemy we would oppress, abuse, and destroy is made in the divine and human image and likeness and is to be treated and welcomed as a neighbor. Indeed, as Great Britain's chief rabbi Jonathan Sacks notes, while the Hebrew Bible has but one commandment to love the neighbor, it includes thirty-six commands to love the stranger.[50] In Deuteronomy 10:18-19 we read that God "shows love towards the alien who lives among you, giving him food and clothing," and that "you too must show love towards the alien." And in Leviticus 19:34 the Hebrews are instructed to treat the alien "as a native born among you" and "love him as yourself, because you were aliens in Egypt."

In the Hebrew Bible two arguments are offered in support of the command to recognize and love the stranger as a neighbor. One set of narratives, found in Genesis 18–19 and 1–2 Kings, suggests that the alien we encounter on the road may be God or an angel of God. Those who recognize and respond to this divine presence masked as a stranger will be blessed with the gift of life, while those who abandon or abuse this alien will suffer death. Another set of texts, found in Exodus, Leviticus, Deuteronomy, and the Prophets, reminds us that the stranger who comes to our door is like our own ancestors, who were themselves unfortunate and mistreated aliens rescued by a God who comes to the aid of such unlucky souls. We are directed to see our own flesh and blood in the faces of the miserable and impoverished strangers before us, and we are to treat them as one of us.

Each of these arguments instructs us to see the unrecognized beauty and humanity of the stranger and does so in a way that parallels the two creation accounts of Genesis 1–2. The first encourages us to find the image and likeness of God hidden beneath the strange face of the alien and warns us that we shall lose our own humanity (or life) if we fail to do so. The second calls us to recognize and treat this stranger as bone of our bone and flesh of our flesh, for in God's eyes these aliens are no different from our own flesh and blood.

[50] Barbara Brown Taylor, "Guest Appearance," *Christian Century*, September 20, 2005, 37.

In Genesis 18:1-15 Abraham and Sarah welcome three strangers approaching their tent in the noonday heat; they offer their guests a shady place to rest, water to wash off the dust of the road, and a sumptuous meal. One of these three strangers turns out to be God, who rewards Sarah, ninety years old and barren, with a child. A life is given for showing hospitality to strangers.

When the two angels accompanying God travel on to Sodom, they are treated monstrously, and the Sodomites are appropriately punished (Gen 19:1-4). Abraham's nephew Lot—himself a resident alien in the city—greets the two travelers at the city gate and invites them to his house for dinner and a night's rest, but after supper Sodom's entire male population comes pounding at Lot's gate, seeking to gang-rape his guests and threatening the immigrant Lot with even worse treatment for daring to condemn their barbaric inhospitality. Then the mob that does not see the humanity of these strangers is blinded and dispersed by God's angels, and the city is destroyed for having treated these aliens so monstrously.

In 1–2 Kings the strangers receiving hospitality and welcome are not angels but the prophets Elijah and Elisha. Still, by recognizing and responding to these strangers as God's messengers, two foreign women exhibit an extraordinary holiness and humanity and are rewarded with the gift of life.

During a drought God sends on Israel as punishment for King Ahab's sins, the Lord dispatches Elijah to the foreign town of Zarephath, where a poor widow on the verge of starvation agrees to share her last handful of food with the prophet. God rewards this generous hospitality by continuously replenishing her food supply, sustaining Elijah, the widow, and her young son through the drought. And when the woman's child falls ill, the Lord brings the boy back to life (1 Kings 17).

In 2 Kings 4:8-37 the prophet Elisha is offered hospitality by a wealthy Shunammite woman who has her husband build a spare room for the traveling holy man. Like Sarah, this generous host, who is without child and married to a man of advancing years, conceives a son in return for her hospitality. And when this child dies, he is revived by the Lord's servant. Again, recognizing and responding to the presence of God in the stranger merits the gift of life.

Each of the previous narratives calls us to recognize the divine image and likeness in the face of the stranger. But it should also be noted that all of the hosts in these stories are themselves strangers and aliens. Abraham, Sarah, and Lot are aliens in Canaan and Sodom, and the two women offering hospitality to Elijah and Elisha are foreigners. Thus, stories that extol the virtue of recognizing and responding to strangers as God's messengers also portray aliens and strangers as persons of great humanity and holiness.

A second set of narratives instructs the Hebrews to recognize and respond to the beauty and humanity of the stranger because their own ancestors were likewise aliens and foreigners oppressed and abused by their captors and overseers. In Exodus, Leviticus, and Deuteronomy the command to protect and provide for the stranger is repeatedly accompanied by the reminder that "you know how it feels to be an alien; you yourselves were aliens in Egypt." (Exod 23:9). So now the Hebrews are to look upon the stranger in their midst and see in these aliens the faces of their own flesh and blood.

Once the Hebrews have recognized the shared humanity that ties them to strangers, there can be no abuse or oppression of these aliens. As God commands the Israelites in Exodus 22:21, "You must not wrong or oppress an alien; you were yourselves aliens in Egypt."[51] Indeed, the resident alien must receive equal justice and protection from the law, for the Lord tells the Hebrews in Leviticus 24:22, "You must have one and the same law for resident alien and native Israelite."[52] Moses reiterates this command in his instructions to Israel's judges in Deuteronomy 1:16. "Hear the cases that arise among your kinsmen and judge fairly between one person and another, whether fellow-countryman or resident alien."

Exodus, Leviticus, and Deuteronomy include several commands to recognize and respond to the alien as a neighbor. Deuteronomy 24:14 forbids withholding the daily wages of the alien laborer, warning that such injustice against the poor is a sin against God. Deuteronomy 14:28-29 instructs the Hebrews to tithe a portion of their produce so that "the aliens . . . in your settlements may come and have plenty to eat." Leviticus 19:9-10; 23:22 and Deuteronomy 24:19-22 require that harvest gleanings of grain, grapes, and oil be left for the alien, reminding the Hebrews that "you were slaves in Egypt; that is why I command you to do this." And Exodus 20:10; 23:12 and Deuteronomy 5:12-15 demand that the Sabbath rest be extended not only to the members of the Hebrew

---

[51] This command is repeated in Exod 23:9; Deut 24:17; 27:19; Jer 7:6; 22:3; Ezek 22:7, 29; Zech 7:10; and Ps 94:6.

[52] See also Num 15:14-16: "When an alien residing with you or permanently settled among you offers a food-offering of soothing odour to the LORD, he should do as you do. There is one and the same statute for you and for the resident alien, a rule binding for all time on your descendants; before the LORD you and the alien are alike. There must be one law and one custom for you and for the alien residing among you."

household but also to "the alien residing among you." Finally, Deuteronomy 23:15-16 commands that runaway slaves seeking refuge in Israel
are not to be returned to their foreign masters but to be offered safe haven
in whatever Hebrew communities they enter: "You must not surrender
to his master a slave who has taken refuge with you. Let him stay with
you anywhere he chooses in any one of your settlements, wherever suits
him best; you must not force him."

Indeed, along with widows and orphans, strangers are part of a protected class of God's "little ones," and righteous Hebrews must imitate
God's special love for these *anawim* by caring for the foreigner as one of
their own. This inclusion of the stranger reaches its fullest expression in
Ezekiel 47:21-23, where God commands the Hebrews to offer the resident
alien a share in their land.

> You are to distribute this land among the tribes of Israel and assign
> it by lot as a share for yourselves and for any aliens who are living
> in your midst and have children among you. They are to be treated
> like native-born Israelites and receive with you a share by lot among
> the tribes of Israel. You are to give the alien his share in whatever
> tribe he is resident. This is the word of the Lord God.

The stranger is to be protected from abuse and injustice and to be
treated and loved as one of our own because in the face of the alien we
recognize our own flesh and blood. The foreigner may have different
customs and costumes, speak in a strange tongue, eat unfamiliar foods,
and pray to other gods. But underneath all these differences is the face
of one who is like us, of one who is bone of our bone and flesh of our
flesh.

The New Testament

The New Testament continues the biblical call to recognize and respond to the beauty and humanity of the stranger, to welcome and love
the alien and foreigner as one of our own. Again and again in his parables
Jesus summons us to recognize the stranger as a neighbor we care about,
and in his radical table fellowship Jesus befriends and breaks bread with
every measure of outcast. But what is even more striking is that the
gospels portray Jesus himself as an alien and outcast. The Word that
becomes flesh in the incarnation has become the flesh of a stranger, and
unless we recognize and respond to this alien flesh as bone of our bone
and flesh of our flesh, we are lost.

In Luke 10:29-37 a lawyer asks Jesus, "Who is my neighbor?" Who must I love as myself in order to earn eternal life? Jesus responds with a parable about a Samaritan rescuing a man who has been robbed, stripped, beaten, and left by the side of the road for dead. In the story a priest and a Levite pass by the injured man without stopping to help, perhaps because they are not convinced this stranger is a neighbor.[53] But the Samaritan is "moved to pity" at the sight of the robber's victim and lavishes care on this stranger as if he were his own child. Unlike the priest and the Levite, the Samaritan has recognized the wounded man as a neighbor and has been a neighbor to this stranger. And so at the close of this tale in which a despised and unclean foreigner proves himself to be the only true neighbor of the injured traveler, Jesus asks the lawyer his own question: "Which of these three do you think was neighbour to the man who fell into the hands of the robbers?"

The point of this parable framed between two opposing questions seems to be that we prove ourselves to be neighbors when we recognize the stranger as a neighbor, when we are moved with compassion and mercy at the sight of the stranger. We become fully human when we recognize and respond to the humanity of the one others ignore and abuse as an alien, when we see the body of the outcast as our own flesh and blood.

And of course Jesus drives this point home by making the only true neighbor in this tale a loathsome stranger we would have overlooked and ignored, and by making a scholar of the law acknowledge that this Samaritan is in fact a neighbor he should love and emulate. The parable of the Good Samaritan packs a punch because the audience does not recognize Samaritans as neighbors and because the alien whose humanity we did not recognize has now become the paradigm of the neighborliness we are to imitate. "Go and do as he did," Jesus instructs us.

The summons to recognize and respond to the humanity of strangers and outcasts runs through several other parables in Luke. In the parable of the rich man and the beggar Lazarus, the former is condemned for never having recognized as a neighbor the poor man camped at his gate, and even in death the rich man does not see or address Lazarus as a fellow human (Luke 16:19-31). In the story of the Pharisee and the tax collector, the self-righteous Pharisee thanks God that he is not like other men, and he is condemned for this arrogance (Luke 18:9-14). And in the parable of the Prodigal Son, the inhumanity of the older brother is revealed

[53] Philip Esler, "Jesus and the Reduction of Intergroup Conflict: The Parable of the Good Samaritan in Light of Social Identity Theory," *Biblical Interpretation* 8, no. 4 (2000): 337–39.

when he refuses to recognize his own brother as anything more than a stranger or alien (Luke 15:11-32). Over and over in these parables the villains are those who fail to see the stranger before them as bone of their bone and flesh of their flesh.

And in his practice of radical table fellowship Jesus models and extends this summons to recognize the stranger as a neighbor. Over and over he breaks bread with outcasts and dines in the homes of those whose sinfulness and ritual impurity have made them strangers and aliens. He invites himself into homes of tax collectors and allows a woman known to be a public sinner to wash his feet.[54] And in one of Mark's accounts of the miracle of the loaves and fishes, Jesus reaches out to feed Gentiles along with Jews.[55]

The parable of the Last Judgment in Matthew 25:31-46 offers a striking explanation for this call to recognize and respond to the humanity of the stranger. The Son of Man, who has come in his glory, welcomes the righteous into God's kingdom because "when I was a stranger, you took me into your home." Meanwhile, the unjust are sent off to eternal punishment because "when I was a stranger, you did not welcome me." The parable suggests that hidden beneath the face of the stranger is the face of God, and it argues that we are to treat the stranger as a neighbor because the Son of Man has become that stranger.

Indeed, in the gospels Jesus does much more than preach about our duty to recognize and respond to the humanity of the stranger. He becomes the stranger. In the accounts of the his birth, the flight into Egypt, and his arrest, torture, trial, and execution, Jesus the Christ is also Jesus the stranger and outcast. The life of Jesus told in the gospels is a parable about the God who becomes an outcast and a stranger to summon us to recognize the humanity of all strangers and outcasts.

THE NEWBORN CHRIST AS OUTCAST

In Luke's infancy narrative the child Jesus is born in a stable and laid in a manger because there was no room for them in the inn (Luke 2:7). It may be that Bethlehem was overcrowded because of the Roman census, but this birth in a shelter built for animals also points to Jesus' solidarity with countless other strangers driven into hovels, caves, and outbuildings too filthy and disgusting for normal human habitation. In the same

---

[54] Luke 5:27-39; 19:1-10; 7:36-50.

[55] Donald Senior, "The Eucharist in Mark: Mission, Reconciliation, Hope," *Biblical Theology Bulletin* 12 (1982): 69. See Mark 8:1-10.

way Steinbeck's migrant pickers were forced from their homes and pressed into lice-infested tent cities and disease-ridden squatter's camps, or African slaves were quartered in outbuildings and shelters little better than the pens and stables used to house animals, Jesus finds himself in a stable, sleeping in a feeding trough.

The Christ Child born in a manger has joined the ranks of all the strangers and aliens exiled from the warmth and safety of domestic life. He begins life among the homeless, the legions of poor, oppressed, and abandoned unable to find safe, secure, and humane shelter. He is a member of all those living in tent cities, homeless shelters, and refugee and relocation camps; he is born into the ranks of those who sleep in cardboard boxes, on park benches, or curled over heating vents. He is part of a great society of gypsies, travelers, migrants, and hoboes who have no place to lay their head.

In most Christian art the birth of Christ is idealized and romanticized. The stable and manger are transformed into a warm domestic scene, with adoring shepherds and livestock surrounding a peaceful and loving family. Mary and Joseph are serene and protective; their sleeping child rests secure in the warm embrace of this nurturing domesticity. An emperor's child would not be more comfortable, content, or well tended.

We might better appreciate the scandal and sting of the stable and manger if we replaced our Renaissance and baroque images of the nativity with pictures of real homeless women clutching their crying and colicky babies, trying to protect them from the cold, hunger, and disease that stalk them so. In *The Crawlers of St. Giles* the nineteenth-century British photographer and social critic John Thompson shows us an exhausted and impoverished woman huddled on the cold and filthy steps of a workhouse, holding the bundled figure of an infant. In lithographs and sketches like *Poverty*, *Bread!*, and *The Downtrodden* the twentieth-century German expressionist Kathe Kollwitz presents us with frightened, desperate mothers unable to protect their vulnerable children from poverty, illness, or death. And in the photojournalist Dorothea Lange's famous 1936 photograph of the *Migrant Mother* we see a tired dust bowl refugee huddled with three of her children in the flap of a camp tent.

The women in these pictures are frightened, shopworn, and weary beyond their years. Their children are hungry, dirty, and ill-tended, and these families live beyond the warm and cheery fires of domestic life, exiled and crowded into places unfit for the rest of us. Into just such a place does Luke put Jesus, connecting the Christ Child to every other stranger cast outside our homes and seeking shelter on the highways and byways.

In Matthew's infancy narrative the child Jesus and his parents are forced to flee to Egypt in the middle of the night (Matt 2:13-18). Having heard rumors of a threat to his dynasty, Herod plans to murder the child; and when the king learns he has been betrayed by his informants, he orders the massacre of every male infant in Bethlehem and its surroundings. As Matthew notes, the night is filled with the inconsolable sobbing and lamentation of mothers cradling their slaughtered children.

With this narrative Matthew links the Christ Child with the legions of refugees driven out of their homes and countries by violence and injustice. Jesus and his parents have become landless exiles terrorized by a murderous tyrant and afraid to return to their homeland. No longer merely homeless, they have been forced out onto the road and driven beyond the borders of their country into foreign lands where they are unwelcome and treated with suspicion and hostility. The scourge of Herod's violence has made them aliens and foreigners.

In this passage Jesus joins the ranks of the more than thirty million refugees and internally displaced persons who today find themselves uprooted and cast out from their homes and communities by conflict and persecution. Like the millions of people, mostly women and children, driven from war-ravaged nations like Afghanistan, Iraq, Columbia, Sudan, and Somalia, the Christ Child and his parents flee the brutal violence of their homeland, becoming stateless persons like those who are crowded into a thousand camps, centers, and communities scattered throughout neighboring, and often impoverished and unfriendly, states.

Again, traditional religious paintings of this flight into Egypt continue to present the Holy Family as peaceful and serene, often being led on their journey into exile by a smiling cherub. The angst and terror of refugees fleeing horrific violence, or the dread and insecurity of strangers traveling through dangerous country, is not present in most of these paintings. To capture what is actually going on for this family in flight, we should perhaps turn to the photographs of refugees and their camps found on the websites of Oxfam or the United Nations High Commissioner for Refugees. Or we might look into the haunting and heartbreaking faces of landless and refugee children staring back at us in *Terra: Struggle of the Landless* and *The Children: Refugees and Migrants*, two books by the Brazilian photographer Sebastiao Salgado.[56] Here are the fright-

---

[56] Sebastiao Salgado, *Terra: Struggle of the Landless* (London: Phaedon, 1997), and *The Children: Refugees and Migrants* (New York: Aperture, 2005).

ened faces of the strangers whom Jesus and his parents joined in their flight into Egypt.

But Matthew has also linked the Christ Child with the massacred innocents of Bethlehem and the surrounding communities. Like Moses, the child Jesus escapes the murderous slaughter that swallows up all the other infant boys of his community. But these innocent victims are forever a part of his story, part of our story of him. And so this narrative ties Jesus to all the innocents slaughtered and massacred in war and persecution. It binds him to all those rounded up and marched into squares or open fields where they could be killed by machete or gunned down. It connects him to all those herded onto reservations or camps and massacred. It makes him the sibling of every victim of slaughter, ethnic cleansing, and genocide, of all those who have been disappeared and dumped into shallow graves. It renders him the ultimate outsider, the stranger who is to be exterminated.

There are no pious and stoic paintings of the slaughter of the innocents. The mothers in these pictures are not serene or calm. They scream and weep in response to the horror being inflicted on their children. In Giotto's fresco of this massacre, a pile of infant corpses are stacked at the feet of sobbing and screaming mothers. Pieter Brueghel's painting of the slaughter has soldiers tearing infants from their mothers' arms. These are the women and children Jesus has been linked with in Matthew's gospel; these are the strangers and aliens cast into the night to wail and gnash their teeth.

In the infancy narratives of Luke and Matthew, the Christ Child is born a homeless stranger, cast out of the warm embrace of domestic life; he becomes a landless refugee, driven into exile by a tyrant's violence, and is tied to all the massacred innocents slaughtered by senseless and inhuman rage and terror. These narratives recount the birth of the savior—but they also recount the birth of the stranger, the outcast, and the enemy. They identify Jesus as the Son of David, the promised Messiah, the King of the Jews, the savior of his people, and the Son of God. But they also identify him as a stranger and alien from his very birth.

Like Luke's tale of the Samaritan, Jesus' own story is a parable in which the central character summoning us to recognize and respond to the humanity of the stranger is himself a stranger and outcast. The difference is that in Luke's parable we easily recognize the Samaritan as a foreigner and are shocked to discover that he is the consummate neighbor, whereas in the case of Jesus we see him first and foremost as Messiah and Lord and are stunned to discover that he is also a stranger and alien.

But that is exactly the point. The Son of God is a stranger, a foreigner, an outcast, and an enemy. The one who has taken on human flesh and been born in a stable has taken the form of a stranger and refugee. And we cannot recognize this child as the Son of God unless we also recognize his solidarity with every stranger, outcast, and enemy. We cannot love this God who has taken on the flesh of strangers unless we also love every stranger and alien. Otherwise, as John writes in his gospel, we are liars.

THE ADULT CHRIST AS OUTCAST

As already noted, Jesus' radical table fellowship put him in the company of all manner of outcasts and aliens. But this practice of breaking bread with sinners and strangers also rendered Jesus an unclean outcast in the eyes of many of his contemporaries. And so this itinerant teacher who had "nowhere to lay his head" (Matt 8:20) became a stranger to many of his own people because he befriended and ate with aliens and outcasts.[57]

But Jesus is revealed as the ultimate outcast in his passion, death, and resurrection. In his arrest, torture, mock trial, and execution Jesus is mistreated, abandoned, ridiculed, abused, and murdered; he is torn from the safety of civil society and cast into a dark wasteland where he may be abused with every injustice and cruelty. The condemned and crucified Christ is the abandoned, abused, and destroyed body of the stranger no longer recognized as a neighbor.

The arrest and trial of Jesus initiates the process of turning this Galilean rabbi into a nonperson who may be abandoned, tortured, and destroyed. In the dark of night a popular prophet and miracle worker is seized by an armed mob, interrogated until dawn, falsely accused and condemned in the worst sort of show trial, and mocked, degraded, and beaten before being handed over to the occupying forces for execution. During this time the prisoner's terrified friends and followers scatter, deserting the teacher they had hoped was the Messiah and repeatedly denying they ever knew or believed in this stranger.

---

[57] Fifteen hundred years later, the Venetian painter Paolo Veronese felt the sting of this rejection when his canvas of the Last Supper sparked the ire of the Roman Inquisition for including all sorts of foreigners, outcasts, and misfits at the table with Jesus. Even Rome, it would seem, is uneasy with Jesus breaking bread with strangers.

Then the Roman authorities flog the betrayed and abandoned prophet, torture and mock him as they would a captured warlord, and have him executed by crucifixion. Taken outside the city, this insignificant enemy of the state is hung between two other criminals, their tortured and dying bodies exposed to ridicule and circled by hungry dogs and vultures.

To see the nonperson that Jesus has become in the eyes of his captors, we need only pull up the infamous pictures of Iraqi prisoners abused and tortured at Abu Ghraib. In the humiliation and degradation on the faces of these captives, we see the disdain and contempt of the bemused guards who took these snapshots and circulated them on the web as trophies. The men and women who took these photographs did not recognize their prisoners as bone of their bone and flesh of their flesh.

Caravaggio captures the process of rendering Jesus a nonperson in a series of paintings of Christ's passion and death.[58] In unsettlingly realistic portraits we see an ordinary young man taken by force, watch him stripped and brutally flogged, observe him tortured and mocked by his captors, and look on as his half-naked corpse is laid in a borrowed tomb. In this abbreviated Way of the Cross the master of chiaroscuro shows us how a neighbor is turned into a creature who may be put down like a beast and disposed of like a piece of meat.

In his crucifixion the transformation to a nonperson is completed. Like all the other strangers who have been degraded and dehumanized until we can no longer recognize their humanity, Jesus has been rendered ugly by being mocked and vilified as a demon, by being torn from a safe and nurturing environment and cast into the dark, by being stripped, spat upon, and assaulted, by having his flesh shredded and scarred, and by being delivered up for destruction. And in this public execution the flesh of a neighbor is fully transformed into the ultimate stranger, a beast who may be slaughtered without remorse or compunction.

But then Luke has this dying stranger ask God to forgive his executioners because "they do not know what they are doing" (Luke 23:34). Certainly, Jesus' captors, torturers, and killers do not recognize him as the Christ, the Son of God. But even more importantly, they no longer recognize him as their neighbor. In the process of rendering Jesus yet another ugly stranger, of transforming him into a nonperson stripped of beauty and ready for destruction, they have forgotten just who this

---

[58] Caravaggio's paintings of Christ's passion and death include *Taking of Christ*, *The Flagellation*, *Christ at the Column*, *Crowning with Thorns*, *Behold the Man*, and *The Entombment of Christ*.

creature hanging from a cross is, and they have cast away their own humanity.

So it is stunning that in the very moment his humanity has been rendered unrecognizable, in the instant he is being transformed into a nonperson, Jesus proves himself to be the ultimate neighbor by recognizing and responding to the fractured humanity of his executioners. Like the Samaritan in Luke's parable, Jesus the paradigmatic stranger and alien proves himself to be a true neighbor by being moved with compassion at the sight of his own killers. Unlike the older brother in the parable of the Prodigal Son, the crucified Jesus turns to his father and begs mercy for his murderous brothers and sisters.

In the gospels Jesus the stranger summons us to recognize and respond to the beauty and humanity of every unrecognized neighbor, to see through every disfiguring scar and mask with which we seek to blot out the humanity of the stranger. To do this, Christ becomes the stranger, the alien, and the enemy, taking on the foreign and disfigured flesh we no longer recognize as human. And he presents us with a stranger who is, in fact, a better neighbor to us than we have ever been to anyone—thereby destroying the very notion of the stranger. For if the one whom we have made into the ultimate stranger, the one who stands with every stranger and alien and outcast, is also the one who has laid down his life for us as a friend, then the very idea of stranger has been shattered.

So that we never forget that Christ has reconciled us to every stranger and summons us to recognize and respond to the humanity of every alien, outcast, and enemy, the risen Christ is forever marked with the scars of one who has been rendered a stranger. In the resurrection account in John, Jesus bears the marks of the crucifixion, identifying him in his glory with all those unrecognized neighbors who have been rendered nonpersons and outcasts (John 20:24-31). These scars on the risen Christ are a vivid reminder that the resurrected Body of Christ includes the abandoned, oppressed, abused, and destroyed body of every stranger, alien, and enemy. In this resurrected body we are reconciled with all strangers and made one flesh, one body in Christ.

RECOGNIZING CHRIST IN THE STRANGER

Among the early disciples of Christ, hospitality to strangers was seen as an essential virtue. As Christine Pohl notes, "Hospitality to needy strangers distinguished the early church from its surrounding environment," and "offering care to strangers became one of the distinguishing marks . . . of the church."[59] Justin Martyr reports that at the Sunday Eucharist a collection for the poor is entrusted to the bishop, who then "helps . . . strangers sojourning among us."[60] The *Didascalia Apostolorum* instructs bishops to show hospitality to any poor stranger who enters the Eucharistic assembly. "If a poor man or woman should arrive . . . and there is no place for them, then you, the bishop, with all your heart provide a place for them, even if you have to sit on the ground."[61] Jerome tells the clergy of his day to "let poor men and strangers be acquainted with your modest table, and with them Christ shall be your guest."[62]

Indeed, the needy stranger was to be shown hospitality because in the face of these aliens and outcasts, believers were to see the face of Christ. Down through the centuries Christian authors and saints summoned their colleagues and neighbors to recognize the face of Christ in the face of the needy and suffering stranger. "Do you want to honor Christ's body?" John Chrysostom asks. "Then do not scorn him . . . outside where he is cold and naked."[63] "When we serve the poor and the sick," Rose of Lima writes, "we serve Jesus."[64] And Vincent DePaul instructs the Daughters of Charity that they must see God in the faces of the poor.[65] More recently, in their joint pastoral letter on migration the Catholic bishops of Mexico and the United States argue that "the Church in our two countries is constantly challenged to see the face of Christ, crucified and risen, in the stranger."[66]

---

[59] Christine D. Pohl, *Making Room: Recovering Hospitality as a Christian Tradition* (Grand Rapids, MI: Eerdmans, 1999), 33.

[60] Justin Martyr, *First Apology 67.7*, in *St. Justin Martyr: The First and Second Apologies*, trans. Leslie William Barnard, Ancient Christian Writers 56 (New York: Paulist Press, 1997), 71.

[61] *Didascalia Apostolorum* 12, cited in William R. Crockett, *Eucharist: Symbol of Transformation* (Collegeville, MN: Liturgical Press, 1989), 255.

[62] Jerome, "Letter 52: To Nepotian," in *Select Letters of St. Jerome*, trans. F. A. Wright (Cambridge, MA: Harvard University Press, 1954 [1933]), 217–19.

[63] John Chrysostom, "Homily on St. Matthew" (*Hom.* 50:3–4, *PG* 58, 508–9), in *The Liturgy of the Hours for the Roman Rite* (New York: Catholic Book Publishing Co., 1975), 182.

[64] *Catechism of the Catholic Church*, 2nd ed (Washington, DC: United States Catholic Conference, 2000), no. 2449.

[65] Vincent de Paul and Louise de Marillac, *Rules, Conferences, and Writings*, ed. Frances Ryan, DC, and John Rybolt, CM, The Classics of Western Spirituality (New York: Paulist Press, 1995), 204.

[66] United States Conference of Catholic Bishops and Conferencia del Episcopado Mexicano, Strangers No Longer: Together on the Journey of Hope (Washington, DC:

Conclusion

According to Genesis, we become fully human when we recognize and respond to the humanity of the stranger, when we see the alien and outcast before us as bone of our bone and flesh of our flesh. And we descend into the worst sort of inhumanity when we fail to recognize our ties to the stranger and set out to transform this unrecognized neighbor into an ugly beast we can abandon, abuse, and destroy. Rendering the stranger ugly is an act of dehumanizing and degrading violence that robs both of us of our humanity.

A chorus of biblical voices summons us to recognize and respond to the dignity and humanity of the stranger and to welcome and tend to this unrecognized neighbor as one of our own. For the stranger and alien is made in our image and likeness, fashioned of our flesh and bones, and shares with us the image and likeness of God. In the face of this alien and outcast, we are to see our own beloved ancestors and children and to recognize the suffering and alienation experienced by our own people. And in these strangers we are to see the image of the God who has a special love for the outcast and alien, as well as the Christ who became a stranger and outcast to reconcile us to one another.

The work of justice begins with the recognition that the one we see as a stranger, alien, and outcast is a neighbor, sibling, and friend. It starts by rejecting every effort to render our unrecognized neighbor as an ugly beast and to remember that this beautiful stranger is indeed, bone of our bone, and flesh of our flesh.

United States Conference of Catholic Bishops, 2003), no. 40.

Chapter 4

Tending Eden's Beauty:
The Human Calling to Care for Creation

A thing is right when it tends to preserve the integrity, stability, and beauty of the biotic community. It is wrong when it tends otherwise.

—Aldo Leopold, *A Sand County Almanac*

Called by Beauty

Over a half century ago Lynn White leveled his "ecological complaint" against Christianity, arguing that the Christian faith bore "a great burden of guilt" for the planet's unfolding ecological crisis because it had long taught believers that nature existed only to serve humanity.[1] As White saw it, the command in Genesis 1:28 to subdue and conquer the earth and to rule over all other creatures had led countless generations of believers to view nature instrumentally and economically as consumable, disposable, and decidedly private property. The biblical instruction to "exercise dominion" gave believers a divine calling to plunder a seemingly limitless bounty of natural habitats, with little or no consideration

---

[1] Lynn White, "The Historical Roots of Our Ecological Crisis," *Science* 155 (March 10, 1967): 1203–7; see also James Nash, *Loving Nature: Ecological Integrity and Christian Responsibility* (Nashville, TN: Abingdon, 1991), 68–74.

of the intrinsic worth of other creatures. Ultimately, of course, this theology of dominion helped bring about a global ecological crisis undermining and unmaking the very work of creation.

In the past half century many Christian churches have responded to this ecological crisis by reinterpreting the biblical command to exercise dominion in ways that highlight humanity's calling to respect and care for the dignity and integrity of all creation. Theologians, pastors, and official church documents stress the sanctity, sacramentality, and intrinsic goodness and dignity of all creation and reframe humanity's ecological vocation in terms of stewardship and kinship.[2] The United States Catholic bishops argue in their 1991 pastoral letter Renewing the Earth that "the human family is charged with preserving the beauty, diversity, and integrity of nature, as well as with fostering its productivity."[3] The Evangelical Lutheran Church in America notes in their 1993 social statement "Caring for Creation" that humans are God's stewards, "called to care for the earth as God cares for the earth, . . . to serve and keep God's garden, the earth, . . . [and] to live according to God's wisdom in creation."[4] And in his 2010 World Day of Peace message Pope Benedict XVI notes that humans have "a duty to exercise responsible stewardship over creation, to care for it and to cultivate it."[5]

Still, as many Christian pastors and theologians have noted, shifting from an instrumental and economic view of nature, which sees humans as lords and masters entitled to conquer and subdue the rest of creation, requires a radical conversion.[6] Recognizing and embracing humanity's

---

[2] Elizabeth A. Johnson, *Women, Earth, and Creator Spirit* (Mahwah, NJ: Paulist Press, 1993), 29; Michael J. Himes and Kenneth R. Himes, OFM, "Creation and an Environmental Ethic," in *Fullness of Faith: The Public Significance of Theology* (Mahwah, NJ: Paulist Press, 1993).

[3] United States Catholic Conference, Renewing the Earth: An Invitation to Reflection and Action on the Environment in Light of Catholic Social Teaching, II.A.

[4] The Evangelical Lutheran Church in America, "Caring for Creation: Vision, Hope, and Justice," September 1993, 2–3, http://www.elca.org/What-We-Believe/Social-Issues/Social-Statements/Environment.aspx.

[5] Benedict XVI, If You Want to Cultivate Peace, Protect Creation, World Day of Peace message, January 1, 2010, no. 13.

[6] Archbishop of Canterbury, "Renewing the Face of the Earth: Human Responsibility and the Environment," March 25, 2009, no. 2, http://www.archbishopofcanterbury .org/articles.php/816/renewing-the-face-of-the-earth-human-responsibility-and -the-environment; John Paul II, Peace with God the Creator, Peace with all of Creation, January 1, 1990, no. 13; United States Catholic Conference, Renewing the Earth, V.C.

ecological vocation to tend and care for all of creation as stewards and servants and kin, along with our calling to recognize, respect, and protect the dignity, integrity, diversity, and sustainability of other creatures and their habitats and ecosystems, demands massive changes in the ways we humans see our world and act in it, and these changes will involve significant, difficult, and decidedly unwelcome sacrifices.

We might seek to bring about this change of heart by pointing out the folly of unfettered dominion. An instrumental and economic view of nature has brought about an escalating global environmental crisis threatening us with a host of cascading ecological catastrophes, including, to mention just a few, this litany offered by Pope Benedict XVI: "climate change, desertification, the deterioration and loss of productivity in vast agricultural areas, the pollution of rivers and aquifers, the loss of biodiversity, the increase of natural catastrophes and the deforestation of equatorial and tropical regions."[7] In addition, the current model of human dominion is contributing to the creation of millions and millions of environmental refugees driven from degraded and exhausted habitats, an increasing presence and threat of conflict and war over access to natural resources, and the most massive extinction of species in sixty-five million years. To cite Hosea 4:3, the fruit of this unsustainable and self-destructive human dominion over nature is that "the land will be desolate and all who live in it will languish, with the wild beasts and the birds of the air; even the fish will vanish from the sea."

Or we might offer a series of ethical arguments to bring about the needed conversion. We could argue, as Catholic Social Teaching has, that the respect for life should be extended to the rest of creation; all creatures and ecosystems have a certain inherent and God-given worth or dignity because they are fashioned and blessed by the Creator and manifest God's glory and grace individually and communally.[8] We might even argue, as John Muir and Peter Singer do, that other creatures have certain rights and that we are obliged as moral beings to respect and protect those rights.[9] Or we might contend that distributive justice, the universal purpose of created goods, a preferential option for the poor, and a basic right to a safe environment oblige us to restrain our use and consumption

---

[7] Benedict XVI, If You Want To Cultivate Peace, no. 4.

[8] United States Catholic Conference, Renewing the Earth, III.

[9] J. Baird Callicott, "Wetland Gloom and Wetland Glory," *Philosophy and Geography* 6, no. 1 (2003): 36; Peter Singer and Jim Mason, *The Ethics of What We Eat: Why Our Food Choices Matter* (Emmaus, PA: Rodale Books, 2007), 241–48.

of nature, to tend and care for creation, and to live more simply so that all people everywhere may simply and safely live. We could also argue that the planetary common good, the biblical commands to exercise stewardship, and the classical virtues of prudence and temperance oblige humans to preserve and protect the natural inheritance of future generations of humans, to make sure all our grandchildren and their grandchildren will have clean air and water, good land, and a rich, integral, and sustainable environment.[10]

Or, taking a different approach, we could appeal to beauty. For while rational and ethical arguments may help bring about the necessary conversion and awaken us to our ecological vocation, beauty also has a special power to change and enlarge hearts and to motivate us to care about and act on behalf of a world that is larger than and creatures that are different from ourselves. Indeed, as Jay McDaniel notes, "When it comes to what motivates people at a deeply emotional level and gives people a sense of meaning, there is a special power in beauty that is not always found in 'truth,' when truth is reduced to merely accurate ideas, or in 'goodness,' when questions of goodness are reduced to matters of abstract 'principles' and 'rules.'"[11] For McDaniel, beauty has more power to move us than reason or ethics alone; and although "moral exhortation and warnings of disaster" have a real place in calling humans to embrace their ecological vocation to care for the earth, we should not "neglect a more joyful and aesthetic approach."[12] The God who created our world and summons us to be stewards and servants is not merely a lawgiver but also "an indwelling lure toward beauty."[13] We need to see and respond to the beauty of creation and the joy, pleasure, and merrymaking of a sustainable life; for it is this lure toward beauty and this joy and merrymaking that will transform and animate our hearts and make creation sustainable.[14]

Therefore, it should not surprise us that, as J. Baird Callicott notes, "historically, many more of our conservation and preservation decisions have been motivated by beauty than duty,"[15] or that, as Ned Hettinger

---

[10] United States Catholic Conference, Renewing the Earth, III.

[11] Jay McDaniel, "God, Sustainability, and Beauty," in "Religion and Environment," ed. Ronald A. Simkins, Supplemental Series 3, *Journal of Religion and Society* 10 (2008): 110.

[12] Ibid., 117.

[13] Ibid., 113.

[14] Ibid., 117.

[15] J. Baird Callicott, "The Land Aesthetic," in *Companion to a Sand County Almanac: Interpretive and Critical Essays* (Madison WI: University of Wisconsin, 1987), 158.

argues, natural beauty and the beauty of animals have been "a major justification for environmental protection."[16] Callicott believes this is because "duty is demanding—often something to shirk; [while] beauty is seductive—something to love and cherish."[17] But it may also be that, as Elaine Scarry, Iris Murdoch, and Simone Weil contend, beauty "unselfs" and "decenters" us with a joyful call summoning us beyond our daily routines and narcissistic concerns.[18] For Scarry, beauty is sacred and unprecedented, wondrous and surprising, and the encounter with beauty awakens within us a joyous attention to and care for the larger world, as well as a deep desire to imitate and recreate the beauty that has so amazed us.[19] John O'Donahue echoes Scarry when he notes that the Greek word "for 'the beautiful' is *to kalon*. It is related to the word *kalein*, which includes the notion of 'call.' When we experience beauty we feel called. The Beautiful stirs passion and urgency in us, and calls us forth from aloneness into the warmth and wonder of an eternal embrace."[20]

Borrowing from Alfred North Whitehead, McDaniel suggests that beauty unselfs and decenters us so joyfully because there is within all creatures an indwelling lure for beauty; indeed, McDaniel and Whitehead believe God is that indwelling lure for beauty within us all. Beauty awakens within us a calling to wholeness, a summons to become whole and relational persons-in-community who are not isolated prisoners trapped within the narrow boundaries of our skin or so-called individual self-interest, but joyous social beings living and working and playing in harmony with and within a larger world.[21] For McDaniel, beauty is the summons to recognize and embrace a larger, more relational self, a self that transcends the fractured boundaries of our narcissistic individualism.

Taking a page from Bruce Benson, McDaniel argues that the indwelling lure for beauty calls us to embrace a vocation to live as artists and musicians in the world, to dwell musically in the world.[22] For the God who

[16] Ned Hettinger, "Animal Beauty, Ethics, and Environmental Preservation," *Environmental Ethics* 32 (Summer 2010): 115–34.

[17] Callicott, "The Land Aesthetic," 158.

[18] Elaine Scarry, *On Beauty and Being Just* (Princeton, NJ: Princeton University Press, 1999), 112–13.

[19] Ibid., 28–30.

[20] John O'Donahue, *Beauty: The Invisible Embrace* (New York: HarperCollins, 2004), 13.

[21] McDaniel, "God, Sustainability, and Beauty," 117.

[22] Ibid., 110.

dwells within us as a lure for beauty calls us to be musicians playing in a jazz ensemble—artists who listen deeply to the harmonies and sufferings of all creation, who find beauty in every note, chord, and melody, and who learn to play together in a way that preserves and renews that rich, often hidden beauty.[23]

Gus diZerega agrees that the beauty of the natural world is the primary motivation behind ecological sensibilities, and he argues that beauty draws humans beyond a narrow, calculating self by awakening a larger, more relational, sympathetic, and authentically human self.[24] For diZerega, our truest self is not individual but relational and compassionate, and the unique character of the human person is found in our ability to step outside our individual selves and imaginatively take up the perspective of the other (human or not).[25] Humans may be responsible for the extinction of many species, but we alone mourn their absence; and it is that sympathy, often awakened by nature's beauty, which makes us most profoundly human. So, without speaking of a vocation to care for creation's beauty, diZerega suggests that humans realize their most authentic selves by reaching out to others (humans and nonhumans) and that this uniquely human sympathy and compassion is often provoked by our sensual encounter with the natural world and natural beauty.[26]

In this way McDaniel, Callicott, and diZerega eschew using ethics or moral norms to press us to tend and care for the earth, taking up instead the call and lure of beauty to persuade us to embrace our ecological vocation as members and stewards of creation. They prefer to offer us, as Callicott would describe it, a "land aesthetic" instead of a "land ethic."[27] And that is the argument offered in this chapter as well, suggesting that humans have a deep and joyous calling to recognize, tend, and care for the beauty of all creation, that we have a vocation to be

---

[23] Ibid., 116 and 127.

[24] Gus diZerega, "Empathy, Society, Nature, and the Relational Self: Deep Ecology and Liberal Modernity," *Social Theory and Practice* 21, no. 2 (Summer 1995): 239.

[25] Ibid., 251–53.

[26] Ibid., 255–57.

[27] Indeed, while it depends largely upon moral arguments in making the case for environmental justice, Catholic Social Teaching also relies upon the beauty of creation as a way of opening our hearts to our ecological vocation to care and tend for the earth. See Benedict XVI, If You Want To Cultivate Peace, nos. 2 and 13; John Paul II, Peace with God the Creator, no. 14; United States Catholic Conference, Renewing the Earth, IV.A.

artists and musicians made in the image and likeness of a creator, restorer, and lover of beauty, and that deep within us dwells an unquenchable thirst for beauty and a hunger to recognize, become, and contribute to the beauty of the whole world. Even more, this chapter suggests that we can find a land aesthetic embedded in the very creation accounts in Genesis that Lynn White used to launch his ecological complaint against Christianity. For in the two creation narratives of Genesis 1–2, we discover an aesthetic argument awakening us to the beauty and intrinsic value of all of creation and summoning us as creatures who make up a small part of this larger masterpiece of beauty to imitate the artist who creates, restores, and delights in this wondrous and unfolding work.

A Land Aesthetic

In his 1949 conservation classic, *A Sand County Almanac*, Aldo Leopold sought to awaken readers to their ecological and ethical calling to respect and care for the natural world, transcending a narrow anthropocentric and utilitarian perspective that viewed other creatures and nature as mere property. To this end Leopold offered a series of moral and scientific arguments for a land ethic that would "enlarge the boundaries of the community [to which humans belong] to include soils, waters, plants, and animals, or collectively: the land."[28] But readers of *A Sand County Almanac* were also most assuredly struck and moved by the beauty of the natural world Leopold introduced them to, an all-too-often unseen or overlooked beauty embedded in creatures and habitats previously considered plain, common, or even dreary. And these same readers were certainly infected by Leopold's contagious delight in what was for them a newly discovered and expansive natural beauty, drawn in by the palpable wonder, awe, and affection he felt in response to the beauty of all things great and small. For Leopold's prose is a sonnet of praise and exultation sung in admiration of a deeply embedded beauty in all the simple, small, ordinary creatures of nature, and of the overarching beauty of the integral, symphonic communities that make up their habitats and ecosystems.

---

[28] Aldo Leopold, *A Sand County Almanac: With Essays on Conservation from Round River* (New York: Oxford University Press, 1966 [1949]), 239.

Because Leopold's ecological calling relies so heavily on awakening readers to the rich and previously unnoticed beauty of much of the natural world, Callicott argues that *A Sand County Almanac* provides us with a land aesthetic as original and revolutionary as the land ethic found there.[29] For by encouraging his readers to look at the natural world through a conservationist lens informed by the insights of evolutionary and ecological science, Leopold invites them to experience and be moved by a natural beauty much richer and broader than the prettiness of isolated mountain scenes, waterfalls, or ocean sunsets.

Callicott describes Leopold's land aesthetic as original and autonomous because it does not reduce nature's beauty to the prettiness of a scenic landscape or a stunning vista, nor does it limit our ecological vocation to preserving those places and creatures whose beauty is immediate and accessible. For Leopold, the natural world is not a two-dimensional painting to be viewed in a museum but a three-dimensional, evolving, diverse, and sensual world in which we are immersed and whose full and often hidden beauty we can only grasp by employing our mind and all our senses.[30]

Western philosophical thought typically paid little attention to nature's beauty, and Westerners generally abhorred the wildness of undomesticated places before the late eighteenth century, when artists began painting landscapes of mountainous scenes, waterfalls, and other striking and extraordinary natural scenery. Suddenly, many wild and remote parts of nature were seen as beautiful, but only to the degree that these places looked like the pretty scenery in landscape paintings.[31] In the nineteenth century, American painters associated with the Hudson River School, like Thomas Moran and Albert Bierstadt, traveled to remote western sites like Yosemite, Yellowstone, and the Grand Canyon and created massive, breathtaking, and hugely popular landscapes of these wilderness areas, no doubt contributing to subsequent preservation efforts that set aside these and other scenic places as national parks and preserves. However, the love of nature generated by these artistic works was not universal. Swamps, wetlands, deserts, prairies, plains, savannahs, and barrens were usually not seen as beautiful (or worth preserving), because they lacked the color or contrast of a mountain lake or waterfall.[32]

---

[29] Callicott, "The Land Aesthetic," 157.

[30] Ibid., 162.

[31] Ibid., 159–60; Callicott, "Wetland Gloom and Wetland Glory," 33–34.

[32] Callicott, "Wetland Gloom and Wetland Glory," 40–42.

Until (and, to a large degree, after) Leopold, conservationists and environmentalists continued to rely on this derivative and self-referential natural aesthetic to persuade the public to protect various species and environments or to pass environmental laws. Voters and donors have generally been moved to support ecological efforts by being shown the wondrous beauty of a specific creature or habitat.

Callicott suggests that Henry David Thoreau and John Muir were early exceptions to this rule, arguing in defense of wild places and species that the general public saw as plain or even ugly.[33] Indeed, Muir offers a religious argument that so-called ugly places (like swamps) and creatures (like crocodiles) possess a beauty in their Creator's eye and plan, even if our narrow human perspective finds this hard to see.[34] In this Muir echoes Chrysostom, Augustine, and Aquinas, each of whom argued that all creatures possess an intrinsic worth and beauty in the eye of the Creator.[35] Indeed, when defending the beauty of maggots and flies, Augustine argued that "every creature has a special beauty proper to its nature, and when a man ponders the matter well, these creatures are a cause of intense admiration and enthusiastic praise of their all-powerful Maker."[36] Still, among modern conservationists, Thoreau and Muir were definite outliers in their defense of the beauty of plain and ugly creatures and habitats.

The problem with a derivative natural aesthetic was that it only saw the beauty of that small segment of nature that resembled pretty scenery and stunning works of landscape art. This beauty was too small, shallow, and self-referential; and if we were ever to be awakened to the full breadth of our ecological vocation, it would be necessary to recognize and be moved by the beauty of all creation, not just a handful of creatures and habitats.

Leopold developed an autonomous land aesthetic that transcended the limits of pretty scenery, that did not stand outside of nature and observe it as a two-dimensional work of art, but immersed us in the three-dimensional world of nature and employed all our senses. In this land aesthetic we not only saw what was pretty but could also hear, feel,

---

[33] Ibid., 35–38.

[34] Ibid., 37.

[35] Jame Schaefer, "Valuing Earth Intrinsically and Instrumentally: A Theological Framework for Environmental Ethics" *Theological Studies* 66, no. 4 (2005): 786–89.

[36] Cited in Arthur Ledoux, "A Green Augustine: On Learning to Love Nature Well," *Theology and Science* 3, no. 3 (2005): 334.

smell, and taste the pleasures and enjoyments of nature. In addition, this authentic natural aesthetic employed the full capacities of human cognition to discover, recognize, and savor a deeper ecological and evolutionary beauty of species and environments.[37] Instead of just catching the surface beauty of isolated pockets of pretty scenery, Leopold encouraged his readers to view all nature through the overlapping lenses of ecology, biology, botany, history, paleontology, geology, and biogeography, enabling us to perceive and enjoy a previously unnoticed complexity, diversity, interdependence, and fitness characterizing so many supposedly plain or common creatures and habitats. Informed by these ecological and evolutionary lenses, Leopold's readers could now appreciate a depth of natural beauty unavailable to those who only looked for a flash of color or a striking composition.

In this way Leopold's autonomous land aesthetic takes all of nature seriously and uncovers the deeper, richer beauty of ordinary and even unattractive places like swamps, barrens, and bogs. But even more, by presenting nature as a three-dimensional masterpiece in which humans are deeply and irretrievably immersed as citizens of a larger community, Leopold's land aesthetic invites readers to "think like a mountain," to see the world and its beauty through eyes much larger than our own, to catch the wonder of its grandeur from a frame far beyond our own narrow utilitarian concerns.[38] Leopold's land aesthetic expands our sympathetic imagination and renders us more humane by letting us see the hidden beauty of a larger world and perspective.[39] In the language of Scarry and others, this land aesthetic unselfs and decenters us.

Of course, such a land aesthetic must be a developed taste, for the beauty Leopold finds and praises in all of nature is often hidden from and overlooked by the uninitiated. As he notes, "In country a plain exterior often conceals hidden riches."[40] And just as a refined taste for classical music requires an education, so too a refined taste for nature's full beauty demands an education, but an education that is morally and spiritually transformative, that changes our hearts and minds. To move from an easy (and thoughtless) enjoyment of pretty and accessible scenery to the recognition and protection of complex and difficult beauties

---

[37] Callicott, "Wetland Gloom and Wetland Glory," 39, 43–44.

[38] Leopold, *A Sand County Almanac*, 138–39.

[39] DiZerega, "Empathy, Society, Nature," 251–52.

[40] Aldo Leopold, *Round River: From the Journals of Aldo Leopold*, ed. Luna B. Leopold (New York: Oxford University Press, 1953), 33.

requires both a cognitive education and a significant shift in sensibilities. And to move from a derivative aesthetic, which is only interested in nature to the degree that it pleases and entertains us, to an autonomous aesthetic, which recognizes the intrinsic dignity and worth of all of nature, demands a moral conversion. As Callicott says, quoting Leopold, "To get at these hidden riches [of nature] takes more than a gaze at a scenic view through a car window or camera view finder. To promote appreciation of nature is 'a job not of building roads into lovely country, but of building receptivity into the still unlovely human mind.'"[41]

So while the lure of beauty may be the path to awaken us to our ecological vocation, it will not be an effortless journey. Our encounter with natural beauty may, as diZerega and others argue, joyfully unself and decenter us in ways that ethical duties or norms do not. We may feel beauty's lure as an attraction instead of an imposition, as morality often seems to be, and it may awaken a sympathy in us for all that we find beautiful. But the initial attraction of pretty creatures and lovely habitats or of scenic vistas and majestic eagles will not pull us far enough out of ourselves to answer the call to be stewards and kin to all creation. Pets and scenic posters alone will not transform us into environmentalists, or at least not environmentalists willing to take up our ecological cross. Like our moral sensibilities, our sense of beauty needs to be schooled and refined, teaching us to recognize and respond sympathetically to the beauty of creatures less and less like ourselves and to the beauty of habitats that strike us as plain and unattractive. We may have a natural sympathy for and attraction to those to whom we feel closely tied, but this affection and attraction needs to be developed toward those who seem strange and foreign to us.[42]

So Leopold offers us a land aesthetic that recognizes and respects the inherent beauty and value of all the natural world, that moves beyond a self-referential appreciation of the easy and accessible beauty of natural parks to an autonomous natural aesthetic that calls us to use all our senses and sciences to see the deeply hidden beauty of the three-dimensional masterpiece in which we are immersed. He invites us to change our hearts and minds so that we might see the beauty of the common and plain and learn to "think like a mountain."

[41] Callicott, "Wetland Gloom and Wetland Glory," 41.
[42] DiZerega, "Empathy, Society, Nature," 251–54; Callicott, "Wetland Gloom and Wetland Glory," 40.

The Land Aesthetic of Genesis 1–2

After Lynn White's ecological complaint against Christianity, it may seem ironic and problematic to look for a land aesthetic in the first chapters of Genesis, to seek our ecological vocation in the very passages where so many generations of Christian rulers, colonizers, industrialists, and capitalists claimed to find a divine calling to subdue, conquer, possess, use, and consume nature as so much chattel or property. Still, this earlier and widespread reading of "dominion" was always unnuanced and incomplete, failing to reflect or integrate other biblical themes like stewardship or service or to consider the Bible's own scathing and sustained criticism of the worldly dominion exercised by the vast majority of history's lords and rulers. Whatever "dominion" means in Genesis 1:28, it could not be intended to encourage believers to imitate the conquest and subjugation carried out by emperors, kings, pharaohs, and Caesars.

Indeed, if we are able to put aside this long-standing and erroneous reading of the texts and take a long, loving look at the two creation narratives of Genesis 1–2, it may be possible to find in them something of a land aesthetic that summons and moves us to recognize and live out our ecological vocation. If we can look at these old and familiar texts as closely as Leopold looks at the common and plain parts of nature, we may find the lure and calling of nature's beauty, unselfing and decentering us joyfully from the bonds of our narrow and utilitarian concerns. For in these two stories there is an attempt to awaken readers to humanity's divine ecological vocation by doing three things: first, uncovering the beauty of *all* creation; second, locating humanity within the larger masterpiece of creation's beauty; and third, pointing out a deep human vocation to create, restore, and tend to the beauty of creation.

Uncovering the Beauty of All Creation

Jame Schaefer notes that Augustine, Chrysostom, and Aquinas rely in part on the first creation account in Genesis to argue for the intrinsic goodness and worth of all creatures and the superlative goodness of the whole of creation.[43] Elsewhere she reports on a larger group of patristic and medieval Christian theologians who use Genesis 1:1–2:4 to affirm

---

[43] Jame Schaefer, "Valuing Earth Intrinsically and Instrumentally," 786–88.

the intrinsic beauty of all God's creatures and the even more sublime beauty of a harmonious and diverse universe.[44]

These theologians turn to this biblical account to argue for the intrinsic goodness and beauty of all creatures and creation because Genesis 1:1–2:4 describes how God creates, blesses, and delights in the beauty of every creature and of the wondrous masterpiece known as creation. Just as Leopold discovers the deeper beauty of nature by looking to its ecological fitness and complexity and evolutionary diversity and depths, the religious authors of Genesis 1–2 find a deeper beauty in all of creation (including its humblest and plainest parts) by pointing to its divine origin and blessed fruitfulness and to the wondrous delight it gives God.

GENESIS 1:1–2:4

Walter Brueggemann once described Genesis 1 as a liturgical poem, and Ellen Davis suggests we can catch the poem's central rhythm in the oft-repeated refrain "And God saw that it was good." Between the fourth and final verse of chapter 1, the poet repeats some version of this refrain seven times, culminating with the enthusiastic report that "God saw all that he had made, and it was very good" (Gen 1:31).[45]

The biblical poet is certainly making an aesthetic judgment about all of creation in this oft-repeated refrain. For in telling us over and over that God saw that it was good, we are being instructed that every creature and the whole masterpiece of creation gave pleasure in being seen, and this is the definition Aquinas offers for beauty.[46] Beauty is that which delights the beholder, and in Genesis 1 creation offers her beholder a sevenfold delight.

But the sevenfold refrain making up the central rhythm of this liturgical poem does more than indicate that creation gives pleasure on being seen; it reports—over and over—that *God* saw that creation was good. By repeating this line again and again, the biblical poet is calling attention to the distinctive way God sees the world and inviting us to savor and delight in creation with the same divine and wonder-filled eyes. In

[44] Jame Schaefer, "Appreciating the Beauty of Earth," *Theological Studies* 62, no. 1 (2001): 26.

[45] Ellen F. Davis, *Scripture, Culture, and Agriculture: An Agrarian Reading of the Bible* (New York: Cambridge University Press, 2008), 43–45.

[46] Wladyslaw Tatarkiewicz, "The Great Theory of Beauty and Its Decline," *The Journal of Aesthetics and Art Criticism* 31, no. 2 (Winter 1972): 166.

this constant refrain we are being encouraged to reach out and catch the divine Creator's infectious awe and delight before the unrecognized and overlooked beauty and goodness of all creation.

By seeing the beauty and glory God sees in this fresh, unfolding creation, we are pulled out of ourselves (and our narrow utilitarian judgments about nature) and come to love what we now see fresh with our own "God-taught" eyes.[47] Watching God delight in creation's beauty, we "catch" this appreciation and beauty and fall in love with the world ourselves. As Augustine argues, if we can see the world as God sees it, we will recognize its wondrous goodness and beauty.[48]

At the same time, in this lyrical narrative we see the beauty in which the biblical author, an agrarian poet, delights. This is not the artistic beauty of a museum painting or even a pretty landscape, but the beauty of a rich and abundant creation well and amply stocked with everything human and other communities will need to flourish and sustain themselves.[49] The term this poet uses to describe God's creative activity is *bara'*, which can mean to fatten or ripen. And in the creation account in Genesis 1, God has created a fat, ripe world, where sunlight, shade, fresh water, good land, and every type of flora and fauna are abundant and plentiful; where a rich, loamy, and well-watered earth sprouts out every kind of sprout; where plants seed every sort of seed; and where a riot of fruit trees bear bounteous fruit with countless seeds for endless generations of future trees, fruit, and seeds.[50] In this wondrous place, the biblical author sees no desperate need, poverty, hunger, greed, or avarice, but only the rich, overflowing, and sustainable abundance of creation, a creation where every living creature is blessed with ample food and sustained in a spacious and nurturing habitat. This, for this biblical author, is beauty.[51]

In addition, this biblical poet points to the beauty of creation by portraying it as an architectural masterpiece embodying symmetry, proportion, and harmony and by presenting it in a rhythmic and lyrical poem

---

[47] Davis, *Scripture, Culture, and Agriculture*, 45–48.

[48] Arthur Ledoux, "A Green Augustine," 333.

[49] F. Gerald Downing, "Environment, Beauty and Bible," *Ecotheology* 7, no. 2 (2003): 189–90.

[50] Richard H. Lowery, "Sabbath and Survival: Abundance and Self-Restraint in a Culture of Excess," *Encounter* 54, no. 2 (Spring 1993): 147–48; Davis, *Scripture, Culture, and Agriculture*, 48–49.

[51] Downing, "Environment, Beauty and Bible," 197–99.

whose form and prose echoes and signals the beauty it represents.[52] As S. Dean McBride writes, the creation that takes material shape in Genesis 1:1–2:4 is a "palatial abode," which Philo of Alexandria referred to as the highest and holiest temple of God.[53] The beauty of this temple is found in both the structure and the sequence of its design. Out of the ugly chaos of a vast wasteland and murky deep—*tohu wabohu*—God the artist creates the cosmos of a triple-tiered temple reaching from the foundations of the earth to the summit of the skies, a marvelous palace spaciously laid out, sumptuously appointed, and lavishly decorated. (And like the house of the Lord in Isaiah 56:7, this temple will be a house of worship for *all* nations—indeed, for all species.) In two matching sets of three days, God creates and fills three descending layers of water, sky, and land, and then on the seventh day the rest or Sabbath of God becomes the crown or apse of this great work, completing the masterpiece of creation.[54]

Finally, the choice to present the first creation account as a liturgical poem invites readers to join in a communal act of praise and exultation, singing with all the rest of creation a joyful hymn celebrating the beauty and wonder of each and every creature, the wonder and awe of the whole masterpiece of the universe, and the delight this awakens in us and our Creator. The form and rhythm of this liturgical poem allude to and imitate the beauty of its subject, offering the sincerest form of flattery to the Creator of this masterpiece. As Scarry notes, beauty is contagious, and our encounter with beauty inspires us to copy and imitate the beauty we see.[55] So the beauty of this poem points back to, celebrates, and even extends the beauty of all creation.

Everything about this first creation narrative praises the beauty of all creation. In the sevenfold refrain that "God saw that it was good" the biblical poet reminds us of the beauty of every creature and of God's pervasive and contagious delight in this beauty. At the same time, the architectural splendor of this palatial creation and the poetic rhythm of the narrative itself communicate the delight and wonder the biblical author takes in the beauty of all creation. Here is a poem that invites and

---

[52] Davis, *Scripture, Culture, and Agriculture*, 43.

[53] S. Dean McBride Jr., "Divine Protocol: Genesis 1:1–2:3 as Prologue to the Pentateuch," in *God Who Creates*, ed. William B. Brown and S. Dean McBride Jr. (Grand Rapids, MI: Eerdmans, 2000), 11.

[54] Ibid., 12–13.

[55] Scarry, *On Beauty and Being Just*, 3.

helps us to catch the beauty both God and the author see in every part of creation.

What is critical here is that seeing creation as God and the biblical poet see it will change us, for a new way of seeing the world must lead to new ways of thinking, judging, and acting in the world; and taking up the long, loving glance that God and the biblical author cast upon the world will transform our minds and hearts.[56] To put it another way, the God who sees the beauty of creation is also the artist who creates this beauty, and in some intimate way the seeing and creating of beauty are connected. In a similar fashion the poet who catches this divine insight seeks to copy this beauty in the form of a poem. As Scarry notes, seeing beauty inspires us to create, sustain, and protect beauty. So, too, as we begin to see the beauty of creation, this aesthetic impulse will change how we act in the world.

GENESIS 2:5-31

The second creation story also introduces us to a beautiful world, fashioned and transformed by God's loving and watering hand. Just as God has created a palatial temple out of the vast wasteland and chaos of *tohu wabohu* in Genesis 1:1–2:4, God transforms a barren and unwatered earth into a world overflowing with flora and fauna, rich in every sort of mineral and treasure and nurtured by great rivers and tributaries feeding and watering every hill and valley and plain; and at the heart and center of this world of beauty, God plants and tends a lush garden paradise, Eden. Indeed, Eden is the source and summit of this second creation narrative. It is the garden of delight nestled in rich agricultural lands and fed and watered by all of creation, and it is the botanical and zoological nursery that nurtures and supplies all the world's habitats.

But Eden is the heartbeat of this second creation narrative not merely because it is the capstone and nursery of all creation, but also because it is a garden, a work of beauty fashioned by human hands to please and delight and to foster a refreshing rest for the body and soul. Unlike forests, savannahs, plains, prairies, jungles, mountain ranges, or wetlands, gardens are a human artifact, a creation of human design and intellect, a product of human civilization—indeed, of advanced human civiliza-

---

[56] Davis, *Scripture, Culture, and Agriculture*, 47–48.

tions.[57] And unlike farms, orchards, vineyards, villages, roadways, aqueducts, canals, or dams, gardens are fashioned and created primarily to delight the senses and provide contemplative rest for the soul, constructed largely out of the same love of beauty that creates temples, palaces, basilicas, parks, and boulevards.[58]

As Penelope Hobhouse notes in *The Story of Gardening*, while the earliest gardens were merely useful plots producing vegetables and herbs, that soon changed. For nearly five thousand years, advanced civilizations have been enamored of the beauty of gardens and have fashioned them as works of art. First, the Sumerians set aside rich and well-watered preserves as royal hunting parks, which were to become the forerunner of ancient and modern landscaped parks. Then the Egyptians developed walled gardens that were irrigated and cooled with an intricate system of canals, pools, and water features and furnished and decorated with a growing assortment of native and imported plants providing beauty, shade, and rest to their users. In time these lush gardens were adopted by Assyrian, Babylonian, and then Persian rulers, who (through Xenophon and Herodotus) gave us the word *paradeisos* (meaning "to wall around") and began the association of gardens with paradise. According to Hobhouse, these ancient Middle Eastern civilizations "established the whole aesthetic of garden enjoyment, their gardens planned for viewing from shady pavilions, with channels of water and flowerbeds sunk below the path levels for ease of irrigation, their groves of trees laid out in strict rows to facilitate watering."[59]

This fascination with the beauty of gardens continued long after the disappearance of Nebuchadnezzar's hanging gardens of Babylon or Cyrus the Great's gardens in Pasargadae and Persepolis. The Romans decorated their homes and villas with peristyle and landscaped gardens, designing and enjoying them as works of art and oases of beauty.[60] Muslim conquerors of Persia embraced the beauty of the ancient pleasure gardens they found there, and they adopted these lush water gardens throughout their empire, savoring them as a foretaste of paradise.[61] Later, Renaissance artists created domestic and public gardens modeled on the

---

[57] Penelope Hobhouse, *The Story of Gardening* (London: Dorling Kindersly, 2002), 16–29.

[58] Ibid., 8–9.

[59] Ibid., 19.

[60] Ibid., 42–55.

[61] Ibid., 56–60.

villa gardens of Pliny, Cato, and other wealthy Romans. And in time these Roman and Renaissance gardens influenced the rise of English landscape gardens.[62]

For nearly five millennia and in nearly every great civilization, gardens have been seen as works of art and centers of beauty. As civilizations advanced, increasingly lavish and pleasing gardens were fashioned as celebrations of the abundant beauty of nature and creation and as islands and oases of beauty and contemplative rest. This was true of the Sumerian hunting parks, the Egyptian water gardens, the hanging gardens of Babylon, and the pleasure gardens of Persepolis. And it is true of Louis XIV's formal gardens at Versailles, London's Kew Gardens, and Monet's gardens at Giverny.

The vegetable gardens in our backyards give us fresh tomatoes, cucumbers, and herbs, and botanical gardens were once planted mainly for medical and scientific purposes, but we also fashion these places for their beauty and for the delight and respite they offer us. We build gardens, greenhouses, and parks in large part because these shady cathedrals lit by a thousand blossoms and blooms and watered by streams, ponds, and fountains are like music to our souls. Like stepping into a temple or museum, we find in these green palaces a small oasis of beauty that soothes and nurtures us, offering a brief respite from the exhausted places where we have trod so hard and long.

Gardens are a work of art, and in Scripture Eden is that supreme masterpiece of beauty manifesting and celebrating the beauty of all creation, as well as the love of beauty in the heart of its Creator. For Eden is a garden of extraordinary delight, a symphony of beauty nestled in and nurturing God's larger labor of beauty and delight. The word "Eden" refers to a "fertile plain" and echoes the Hebrew term for "delight," so the garden God plants in Eden must be a "garden of delight," a "pleasure park," or a paradise.[63] In this lush garden, God has planted "every kind of tree pleasing to the eye and good for food" (Gen 2:9), producing a cornucopia of delights for the eye and palate. And, like other artistic masterpieces, Eden's beauty overflows its boundaries, breaking out into and nurturing the larger world. The river flowing from Eden and watering its garden feeds the tributaries irrigating the whole world, nourishes

[62] Ibid., 42–47.

[63] See Jack Suggs, ed., *The Oxford Study Bible: Revised English Bible with the Apocrypha* (New York: Oxford University Press, 1992), footnote to Genesis 2:8, p. 12.

lands rich in gold, gum, resin, and cornelian, and feeds the agriculture of all of Havilah, Cush, and Asshur (Gen 2:10-14).

Eden's beauty is not limited to its flowers and trees. For God has also filled Eden with every sort of wild animal and every kind of bird imaginable and brought them before the human to be named. The pleasure park of Eden is not merely a garden but also a zoo and an aviary. Here is a garden with more flora and fauna than any king has ever owned or any zoo has ever kept. Eden is a riot of color and forms, a rainbow of creatures, pressed down and overflowing with bounty and beauty.

The second creation narrative affirms the beauty of all creation, in large part by placing beauty at the very heart of the created world. For the Garden of Eden is the gateway, summit, and source of God's creative activity in Genesis 2:5-31, and this pleasure park is a paradise that gathers in and radiates all the beauty of the world God has formed and fashioned. Making Eden the centerpiece of creation signals the beauty of all creatures and creation. In addition, as we shall see, humans have been placed in this garden to tend and care for this beauty and for the beauty of all the world.

Placing Humans within the Larger Beauty of Creation

Leopold's land aesthetic does not have humans viewing nature's beauty as a two-dimensional landscape painting hanging on a museum wall; rather, it immerses us within the three-dimensional world of nature. Likewise, both creation accounts in Genesis 1–2 advance their land aesthetic by embedding humans within the larger masterpiece of creation, making us works of beauty within a much greater and far more magnificent artistic work. In neither of the two creation narratives are humans external observers of creation's beauty; they are integral parts of this larger masterpiece. In both narratives the beauty of humans is affirmed, but it is a beauty that is grounded in and related to the larger beauty of all creation. The real beauty of humans, as well as their calling to create, restore, and sustain beauty, is to be found in their intimate and integral relationship to the larger work of creation. Creation and nature do not form a backdrop against which we see the unique beauty of humans. Instead, the genuine beauty of humanity is found in our embedded relationship to the larger whole of creation. This is particularly clear in Genesis 1:31, where the divine Creator, completing six days of artistic labor, steps back to admire and delight in this wondrous masterpiece: "God saw *all* that he had made, and it was *very* good" (emphasis added).

In Genesis 1:27 human beings are created in the divine image as male and female, and we know that these humans are beautiful because they are an essential part of the creation in which God so delighted when he saw that it was all very good. We also know of their beauty because they are, as already noted, fashioned in the image and likeness of God, which must certainly point to a delightful form. And we know of their beauty because they are fashioned as a harmonious community of persons ("male and female he created them") that image the larger masterpiece of God's creation. In short, humans are beautiful because they image the Creator of all beauty, because they image the balance and harmony of creation's beauty, and because they are a part of the larger work of beauty that God has found to be so very good.

What is essential here is that humans do not stand outside creation and look down upon it from above. In spite of traditional interpretations of the command to exercise dominion, in Genesis 1:27 humans are created not as lords and masters of the universe but as citizens of a larger community, as members of a great and holistic living masterpiece.[64] In this biblical narrative humans are siblings and kin to the rest of creation, musical notes embedded in a larger symphonic masterpiece, patches of bright cloth woven into a splendid quilt of so many colors.

For in Genesis 1:27 humans are fashioned by the same artist who has created the earth and heavens; they are made by the same hand that has formed the birds of the air, the beasts of the earth, and all the creatures teeming in the seas. And the creation of humans in Genesis 1:27 is part of an infinitely larger project that has parsed day from night, separated water from dry land, decorated the heavens with a cascade of shimmering lights, and filled the earth, sky, and waters with a teeming abundance of life. In addition, the humans fashioned with such loving care in Genesis 1:27 are immediately instructed, as we will see later, to share space and habitat and food with all the other members of this global biotic community, just as they share in the same divine blessings and delight that God showers upon all their companions and fellow creatures. For these humans are siblings and citizens within the universal family of creatures that makes up creation.

Humans are also part and parcel of the larger masterpiece of creation in the story of Eden in Genesis 2:5-31. In this second creation narrative, the biblical author indicates that humans are kith and kin to all other

---

[64] Johnson, *Women, Earth, and Creator Spirit*, 29–30.

creatures by noting that we are made of the same stuff (clay/earth) from which the Creator of this masterpiece of beauty has fashioned all other creatures. In Genesis 2:9 and 2:19 we read that the Lord God fashioned every kind of tree and shrub and grass and all the wild animals and birds of the air out of the same ground used to form the first human in Genesis 2:7. The human flesh and bones Adam recognizes as his own when he first looks upon Eve is, according to the author of Genesis 2:5-31, made of the same biological material filling the cells of the world's flora and fauna, and all of this material ties us to the earth and to what Leopold calls the "land community." Hence, humans have every reason to imitate St. Francis in calling all other creatures their sisters and brothers.

But in Eden humans are not merely made of the same stuff as other creatures. They are called to be in radical communion with other creatures and in harmony with the rest of creation, and any frustration of that communion and harmony warps their very identity as humans. As we will see below, Genesis 2:15 reports that humans have a calling to tend to the beauty of God's creation and are fashioned and placed by God to serve this purpose. So, echoing Gus diZerega's claim that human identity is relational and Jay McDaniel's assertion that a divine hunger for beauty has been placed in the human heart, the second creation narrative describes humans as creatures called to care for and tend to the beauty of creation itself. We are fulfilled as humans and achieve our calling by reaching out of ourselves in caring service of the beauty of creation. We are meant to be a part of and to care for something greater and more wondrous than ourselves.

And we are not, it would seem, meant to be alone. In Genesis 2:18 the Lord God said, "It is not good for the man to be alone," suggesting that such aloneness renders us incomplete, perhaps even inhuman. And so, to complete the creation of our humanity, God fashions every sort of beast and bird as possible companions and invites the human to come to know and name all these fellow creatures. The lesson here, understood by anyone who has ever cared for (or been cared for by) a plant or pet, is that in the larger community of creation humans are much more than cocreatures and caretakers; by our very nature we are companions to all other creatures, and our humanity is diminished when we forget or ignore this.

Like Leopold, the author of the Eden creation narrative sees humans as citizens of a larger land community, people of the soil fashioned of the same earth from which all other creatures are formed, people formed to tend and serve this larger community, people who become fully human through their recognition that they are indeed not alone but in communion with the land, plants, other animals, and other humans.

Created as Artists and Gardeners

The land aesthetic in Genesis 1–2, however, does not merely place humans within the larger masterpiece of creation; these narratives establish that humans have a divine calling as artists and gardeners to create, restore, tend, and delight in the beauty of creation. As we saw in chapter 2, the human desire to create beauty is not the preserve of a small cluster of elite geniuses but a universal human condition, surfacing in every community, age, and place. No matter how difficult or brutal the conditions, no matter how much energy and resources were required to meet the need to survive, humans in every culture and era have fashioned works of beauty. As Nicholas Wolterstorff argues in *Art in Action*, the impulse to create beauty, to exercise the human calling as cocreators of a world of beauty, is not a luxury but a pervasive and fundamental human need.[65] And the two creation narratives of Genesis 1–2 affirm this universal and divine calling to tend and recreate the beauty of creation.

CREATED AS ARTISTS

In Genesis 1:27 humans are created (male and female) in the image and likeness of God. But the God in whose image we are formed is an *artist* who imagines, designs, creates, restores, delights in, and tends to beauty. In this first creation narrative God functions primarily as an artist and architect transforming a desolate and chaotic world shattered by violence and injustice, an exhausted and threatening world rendered barren, wild, and ugly, into a palatial temple lavishly appointed and furnished with every sort of creature and being. The God in whose image and likeness humans are being fashioned has been confronted with the chaos and ugliness of *tohu wabohu*; and in the course of this liturgical poem, this same artist God imagines, designs, and creates (or restores) a world of extraordinary beauty, a lush and harmonious cosmos overflowing with a teeming menagerie of creatures sharing an abundance of food, water, and habitat.[66]

---

[65] Nicholas Wolterstorff, *Art in Action* (Grand Rapids, MI: Eerdmans, 1980), 4.
[66] Lowery, "Sabbath and Survival," 144–46.

This Creator and restorer God is one who feels the lure of beauty in the midst of the rank and impenetrable fog and muck of *tohu wabohu*. This divine artist and architect imagines, designs, and crafts a world overflowing with beauty and savors and delights in this beauty as it unfolds in her creative and artistic hands. Here in Genesis 1:1–2:4 is a divine artist inspired and lured by a dream or vision of beauty, an architect imagining, designing, creating, and restoring beauty, as well as enjoying and delighting and rejoicing in it.

If the cosmos created in Genesis 1:1–2:4 is a palatial temple, the Creator is the artist and architect who has first imagined this masterpiece in an ugly and putrid world exhausted and degraded by injustice, abuse, and violence—a chaotic and inhospitable world. And while other creation myths tell of worlds formed by sacred and redemptive violence, this Creator transforms the waste and ruins of worlds destroyed and exhausted by conquest, greed, and abuse into a work of unimaginable beauty. The Creator described in Genesis 1:1–2:4 is an artist, an architect, who creates, restores, and delights in beauty.

In addition, this God, in whose image and likeness humans are fashioned, is an artist who blesses and liberates the creativity and artistry of her creation, setting creatures and creation free to enrich and add to the beauty she has fashioned. In creation this divine artist has fashioned a living and fruitful masterpiece that shares in, celebrates, and continues her artistic creativity.[67] Moreover, like all other artists who pause regularly to be fed by their muses, this Creator God rests from her labors, pausing to dwell deep in the lure of beauty that abides within her, to drink deeply from the creative rest that will inspire and renew; she blesses this rest as the font of ongoing creation and artistry. This God is no mere laborer or contractor but an artist who imagines, designs, creates, restores, and takes delight in beauty.

Indeed, everything about Genesis 1:1–2:4 suggests that the God who fashions creation is an artist, which means that humans—who are made in the image and likeness of this God—are being fashioned as artists as well. To say repeatedly in Genesis 1:27 that we are made in the image and likeness of God means that humans are fashioned as creators and restorers of a world of beauty; as imaginers and designers and tenders and protectors of the beauty of creation; as artists who rest and renew themselves before taking up again the ongoing and artistic labor of creation;

---

[67] Steven Bouma-Prediger, *For the Beauty of the Earth: A Christian Vision for Creation Care* (Grand Rapids, MI: Baker Academic, 2010), 94.

and as beings whose primary identity and character is to be found in their likeness to the one who has created this world of beauty, whose labor is to create the world, who saw that this creation was good (pleasing to the eye), and who blessed this creation.

If humans are made in the image and likeness of the one who imagined and fashioned creation in response to the lure of beauty and who delighted in each part and in the whole of creation, seeing that every created being was good and that the whole masterpiece was very good, then Genesis 1:1–2:4 suggests that humans image God best when we—like God—can see and be moved by the beauty of creation. What is distinctive about creatures fashioned in the image and likeness of the Creator is the capacity to see and delight in the beauty of *all* creation and to feel a calling to create, restore, and protect this beauty wherever we find it. Thus, in Genesis 1:27 our humanity is to be found in this divine ability to see, be moved by, and tend to the beauty of other creatures and the rest of creation. This parallels McDaniel's claim that God is within us as an indwelling lure of beauty, while diZerega connects our humanity with a unique sympathy with other creatures, a sympathy closely related to our attraction to the beauty of the natural world.[68]

To be made in the image and likeness of the artistic God described in Genesis 1:1–2:4 means that our identity and vocation as humans is wrapped up in being artists in the world, in being creatures who "catch" the way God sees the world, who recognize and respond to the lure of its deep beauty, who care about, restore, and protect the beauty of all creation. Far from being dominators and masters who only see the world instrumentally and economically, Genesis 1:27 suggests we are called to be artists haunted by the world's deep beauty and committed to cocreating, protecting, and restoring this beauty. And so we violate our deepest selves, our divine and biblical vocation, our very humanity, when we engage in practices that unmake creation and advance the ugliness and chaos of *tohu wabohu*.

Along with the assertion of Genesis 1:27 that humans are made in the image and likeness of an artist, we know of our artistic calling to care and tend for the beauty of creation from three sets of instructions found in this first creation narrative. In Genesis 1:28-29 God directs humans to be fruitful and multiply, instructs them regarding the foods they and other creatures are to eat, and commands them to have dominion over

---

[68] McDaniel, "God, Sustainability, and Beauty," 113; DiZerega, "Empathy, Society, Nature," 253.

other creatures. And though it may not seem so at first, these three instructions direct humans to exercise their artistic vocation by caring for and tending the beauty of all creation.

(A) *Share space.* Humans receive a command to "be fruitful and increase" and "fill the earth" in Genesis 1:28, and for centuries Christian colonialists and industrialists have justified the expansion, incursion, and settlement of humans in every habitat and region of the planet, as well as the domestication, deforestation, and desertification of many places, by pointing to this divine command. Indeed, even as the human invasion and transformation of habitats has crowded out countless species and contributed to the greatest wave of extinctions in sixty-five million years, too many Christians have seen this growth as commanded and blessed by the Bible's God of creation.[69]

It needs to be remembered, however, that God's instruction to humans in Genesis 1:28 follows a similar command given to the creatures of the water and sky (Gen 1:22), who are also told to be fruitful and multiply, and only comes after the same Creator God has already filled up the land with all sorts of livestock and wild animals (Gen 1:25) and every sort of vegetation (Gen 1:12). So the command that humans be fruitful and multiply must be read as part of a larger ecological design in which a host of different life forms are blessed with creative fertility and expected, like the children on every playground, to live, work, and play well with one another.

So, although some have read the instruction in Genesis 1:28 to be fruitful and multiply as an unlimited warrant for humans to reproduce and spread, consuming all the planet's resources and exhausting all its habitats, the truth is that this command is part of an overarching vision or ethic requiring that *all* creatures share the world's space and honor each other's habitats. For the command that humans be fruitful and multiply cannot cancel the other commands that plants and animals multiply nor undo God's previous labors of creation. Instead, the command that humans be fruitful and multiply goes along with an implicit command to recognize, respect, and protect the habitats of all other creatures as well. Otherwise, Genesis 1:28 is a command that humans metastasize and colonize and consume all habitats in an annihilating and self-destructive cancer, and this would lead to the unmaking of creation itself.

---

[69] Davis, *Scripture, Culture, and Agriculture,* 53–55.

Therefore, the biblical instruction to be fruitful and multiply and to fill up the earth directs humans to create and protect the most lively, fruitful, and sustainable communities of creatures possible, to encourage and ensure the growth of vital, diversified, and interdependent habitats and ecosystems providing the richest and most sustainable resources and nutrients for every form of life and recycling the waste of all these living creatures into food and nutrients for their neighbors and colleagues.

Instead of being a command simply to multiply humans like widgets in a factory, Genesis 1:28 must be read as a moral instruction to use human creativity and intelligence to support and sustain the most vibrant communities of life possible. Such ecological communities will reflect and be nurtured by the complexity, diversity, harmony and beauty of the larger masterpiece of creation described in Genesis 1:1–2:4, and will be achieved by humans who appreciate, defend, restore, and tend to this larger beauty.

As a result, faithfully following the command to be fruitful and multiply demands that, in order to produce the most fruitful habitats and ecosystems possible, humans must create, protect, and sustain vibrant, diverse, and interdependent communities of life where humans and other creatures share space and resources.

This sharing of space, which contributes to the greatest possible creativity and fruitfulness, is to be contrasted with the colonization of space modeled by monoculture plantations and so-called factory farms purportedly geared to the most efficient production of a single crop or livestock.[70] For in spite of the supposed efficiencies introduced by these mechanized operations, such "farms" create all sorts of harm to animals; undermine and weaken local and regional human communities; produce a rising tide of environmental threats, sickening and endangering local, regional, and global habitats and ecosystems; and significantly reduce the general vitality and health of the planet.[71] In the strictest sense of the term, these plantations may "multiply" the number of bushels of corn harvested or the tally of pigs slaughtered, but they do not produce or sustain fruitful communities or fill up the earth with life.[72]

---

[70] Robert Albritton, *Let Them Eat Junk: How Capitalism Creates Hunger and Obesity* (New York, NY: Pluto Press, 2009), 64–66.

[71] Mark E. Graham, *Sustainable Agriculture: A Christian Ethic of Gratitude* (Cleveland, OH: Pilgrim Press, 2005), 83–93; Singer and Mason, *The Way We Eat*, 42–69.

[72] Davis, *Scripture, Culture, and Agriculture*, 52.

Rainforests may represent the best example of land use that encourages and supports the command to be fruitful and multiply and to fill up the earth with life. But countless living creatures also share space and habitat to their mutual advantage in a variety of earthly habitats, including forests, prairies, savannahs, wetlands, oceans, lagoons, coral reefs, jungles, and deserts, to name a few. And for much of the past ten thousand years, human agriculture in small and medium-sized farms has imitated this dynamic interdependence and increased fruitfulness by fostering cooperation and collaboration among species.

Indeed, though the cost of human labor has encouraged larger and larger mechanized and monoculture farms, small and medium-sized farms with a variety of crops and livestock continue to be more productive per acre and more sustainable in their use of resources than their monstrous monoculture neighbors.[73] Crop rotation, intercropping, and the use of natural pesticides and fertilizers make small family farms more fruitful in their production and sustenance of food, life, and soil and work against the erosion of rural communities, while grain subsidies provided to large agribusinesses foster the unsustainable use of petroleum-based fertilizers and pesticides, the artificial overproduction of monoculture crops, the erosion of topsoil, the pollution of rivers and streams, and the growth of dead zones in coastal waterways.[74] Can this really be fruitful?

Joel Salatin's oft-cited Polyface Farm, described in detail in Michael Pollan's best-selling *Omnivore's Dilemma*, represents the sort of interdependent and sustainable family farm that makes good use of the contributions and resources provided by a variety of crops, grasses, livestock, and other plants and animals sharing the space of Salatin's farm, resulting in a land that is vastly more productive and sustainable than monoculture plantations.[75] Meanwhile, in Cuba a shift from monoculture plantations to small farm cooperatives (*organoponicos*) has significantly increased the agricultural productivity, independence, and sustainability of the island nation and radically improved the vitality and interdependence of farming practices.[76] By learning to share space, labor, and

---

[73] Graham, *Sustainable Agriculture*, 144–45.

[74] Ibid., 137–39.

[75] Michael Pollan, *The Omnivore's Dilemma: A Natural History of Four Meals* (New York: Penguin Press, 2006), 123–33, 208–25.

[76] Graham, *Sustainable Agriculture*, 174–82.

information, Cuban farmers have indeed followed the mandate to be fruitful and multiply.

In light of these points, the command in Genesis 1:28 to be fruitful and multiply and to fill up the earth should be read as an instruction to imitate the artist Creator of Genesis 1 by using human creativity and intellect to encourage and foster the growth of lively, fruitful, and sustainable communities. This instruction opposes the monoculture plantations and factory farms believed to be so good at producing large numbers of crops and livestock but which undermine the vitality, diversity, and sustainability of a host of local, regional, and global habitats and resources.

(B) *Share food.* In Genesis 1:29 God sets aside all seed-bearing plants and fruit-bearing trees as food for humans, and in the next verse God provides a separate portion of all green plants for all wild animals, birds of the air, and things that creep on the earth—indeed, for every living creature. This simple division of foods for humans and all other living creatures cannot represent a complete dietary catalog for the planet's inhabitants, for there is no mention of the living creatures that teem and swarm in the waters and no recognition that humans and countless other animals also eat flesh. Instead, just as God's creative activity had begun with the separation of light from dark in the formation of the first day and night, the separation of the waters above and below the vault of the heavens on the second day, and the separation of the waters below from the dry land on the third day, so too God's creative activity continues here with the separation of food for humans and other creatures on the sixth day. And just as the separation of light and dark, of upper and lower waters, and of land and sea had been part of God's creation of an artistic masterpiece characterized by balance, harmony, and beauty, so too the separation of foods into fair portions for humans and all other creatures is part of God's ongoing creative masterpiece. For as the three separations effected in the first three days of creation overcame the murk and chaos of *tohu wabohu,* so the separation of foods here seeks to overcome another sort of chaos by providing each community of living creatures with a fair and adequate portion.

In these two verses all the plant food produced by the planet is divided into two portions, one for humans and the other for all other living creatures. Humans are instructed to take their food from their portion of seed- and fruit-bearing plants and directed to leave the rest for all other living creatures. The verses work together to instruct humans to share the planet's food supply with all other creatures, to recognize and respect the claim other creatures have on their fair share of the earth's food. These verses give no support to the notion that everything on the planet is for the use and consumption of humans or that other creatures have no claim on creation's bounty.

Just as the command to be fruitful and multiply directed humans to imitate the creative artistry of God by fostering and protecting vibrant, diverse, and sustainable communities of life through the sharing of habitats, so too this instruction dividing food between humans and other creatures directs us to create harmonious and vibrant communities by practicing justice and sharing food with all other living beings.

The sharing of food commanded in Genesis 1:29-30 is aimed at creating a peaceful banquet at which all have enough and no one has too much. In this way these two verses anticipate the sharing of food called for in Exodus 16:17-18, where although some Hebrews had gathered more and others less manna, all found that they had just enough, and none had too much or too little. This division of food also anticipates the fair division of farmland among the Hebrew tribes settling in Canaan in Joshua 13-18, which ensured that every tribe and family received a fair share of the land flowing with milk and honey. And it anticipates the sharing of loaves and fishes among the large crowds who followed Jesus into the wilderness, a sharing that transformed these audiences into peaceful communities where everyone had enough and none had too much to eat.[77]

So, along with carrying out our ecological vocation as artists made in the image and likeness of the God who fashions, restores, and delights in beauty by sharing habitats with other creatures, humans are called to tend and care for the beauty of all creation by sharing food. Indeed, the placement of this instruction suggests that, along with learning to share habitat, sharing food is the primary way humans live out their ecological vocation to tend and care for the beauty of the earth.

Unfortunately, all too often modern forms of human food production do not create more just and harmonious communities or preserve the beauty and harmony of creation. The modern industrial agricultural system formed and fueled by global capitalism has proven singularly inept at ensuring that all have enough and none has too much. Canadian political scientist Robert Albritton reports in *Let Them Eat Junk* that this

---

[77] See the six accounts of the multiplication of loaves and fishes in Matt 14:13-21; 15:32-39; Mark 6:30-44; 8:1-10; Luke 9:10-17; John 6:1-21.

system has led to a world where a quarter of the planet's population are chronically hungry or undernourished, while another quarter are over-nourished and suffering from excessive or unhealthy food consumption.[78] And far from protecting a fair share of food for all living beings, it inflicts widespread and unprecedented suffering on countless millions of livestock animals raised for food, replaces their natural foods with an unsuitable diet of corn, animal byproducts, hormones, and antibiotics, depletes and destroys fishing stocks around the world, wastes up to 40 percent of the food it produces, and pollutes, exhausts, and degrades local and regional environments with unsustainable practices, toxic chemicals, and unrecycled waste.[79] With its reliance on fossil fuels, chemical fertilizers, pesticides, monoculture plantations, Concentrated Animal Feeding Operations (CAFOs), and factory farms, this global agricultural system fails to produce a fair portion of food for half the planet's human population, inflicts suffering and hardships on countless communities of other living creatures, and relies on unsustainable resources.

The direction to share food with all other living creatures reminds humans of our ecological vocation to tend and care for the beauty of creation by ensuring that all God's creatures have the resources and food required to flourish in vibrant and diversified communities of life.

(C) *Have dominion.* As we have already seen, the command in Genesis 1:28 has long been understood by many Christians and their critics as granting humans a lordship over the rest of creation that justifies the seizure, consumption, and destruction of all creatures and habitats, as long as this serves the interest of their human owner and master. Such a command, the popular argument has suggested, permits and encourages any human use, abuse, or destruction of the beauty of creation, which has no inherent value and exists only to serve human purposes.

Still, this directive to exercise dominion "over the fish in the sea, the birds of the air, and every living thing that moves on the earth" must be put in context. On the fourth day of creation God places great lights in the vault of the heavens "to govern" our days and nights, but the rule of the sun and moon is one of service, for they are to announce the festivals, seasons, and years, and to separate our days and nights so that we will have time for work and play and rest. Might not, then, the placing

---

[78] Albritton, *Let Them Eat Junk,* ix.

[79] Ibid., 147–64; Singer and Mason, *The Way We Eat,* 21–68, 111–50, 231–69; Graham, *Sustainable Agriculture,* 83–137; Pollan, *The Omnivore's Dilemma,* 32–57, 65–85.

of humans over other creatures in Genesis 1:28 also reflect a calling to serve the rest of creation? After all, as we will see below, the placing of the humans in Eden in Genesis 2:15 reflects their calling as gardeners to tend and care for the rest of creation.

In addition, we have just been told twice in Genesis 1:27 that these humans are fashioned in the image and likeness of an artist who creates and restores the beauty of a world that was chaos and desolation; and the ancient authors of this text would certainly have known how such desolation and destruction was so often the result of humanity's abuse and exhaustion of the natural world. Indeed, after several thousand years of advanced agricultural empires that repeatedly exhausted and depleted the natural environments that had fed and fueled them or that had destroyed these environments through war and conquest, the biblical authors of Genesis 1 must have suspected that the human dominion exercised by the world's lords and masters had led again and again to its own form of *tohu wabohu*. Is it likely, then, that the Creator and restorer of beauty described in Genesis 1, upon completing and furnishing the palatial temple of this new creation, would direct humans to treat this masterpiece as so much chattel or property and to use and abuse all the creatures in whose beauty God repeatedly delights, as if they were slaves and beasts of an imperial lord? Is it not much more likely that the dominion described in the liturgical poem of Genesis 1:28 is to be understood ironically, as a critique and rejection of the cruel and abusive dominion of worldly kings and rulers, and as a call to imitate the unique lordship of the one who creates and restores and delights in the beauty of all creation? This would mean that Genesis 1:28 tells us that humans have been set over other creatures, just as the sun, moon, and stars have been set over the earth, to serve and protect the masterpiece of creation.

This reading of Genesis 1:28 fits with other biblical texts criticizing the abusive and destructive dominion exercised by agricultural empires and emulated by their subjects and neighbors, and it echoes God's constant reminder to the Hebrews that they are not owners and possessors of their land but stewards holding and caring for Canaan in the name of creation's only master. We find this criticism of ordinary human dominion in the decision not to appoint a king over the Hebrews when they settle in Canaan (Deut 1:13-18) and in the scathing critique of kings offered in 1 Samuel 8:11-18. Here the prophet reminds Israel that kings always end up seizing what is not theirs, conscripting other people's sons and daughters as fodder for their war machine and as slaves for their household, and stealing the best portions and fruit of other people's lands. And in Jeremiah, Hosea, Amos, and Isaiah we find repeated criticisms of the villainy and cruelty of kings, both domestic and foreign. Indeed, the biblical texts are profoundly suspicious and critical of those exercising the world's form of dominion and lordship.

Moreover, any Christian reading Genesis 1:28 has even more reason to interpret this instruction ironically and to reject any command to exercise lordship over creation as the world's empires and rulers do. For Christians, the notion of dominion must be shaped by Christ's understanding of lordship, which is radically different from—even the polar opposite of—the common understanding of dominion. In Mark 9:33-37 Jesus reprimands the disciples for their ambition to rule over one another, telling them that "if anyone wants to be first [in the reign of God], he must make himself last of all and servant of all." And in Matthew 20:25-28 Jesus instructs the Twelve to reject the worldly model of dominion, telling them instead that "whoever wants to become great must be your servant, and whoever wants to be first must be the slave of all— just as the Son of Man did not come to be served but to serve, and to give his life as a ransom for many." So too in the Last Supper account of Luke 22:24-27, Jesus reminds the Twelve that "Among the Gentiles, kings lord it over their subjects; . . . Not so with you: on the contrary, the greatest among you must bear himself like the youngest, the one who rules like one who serves. For who is greater—the one who sits at table or the servant who waits on him? Surely the one who sits at table. Yet I am among you like a servant." And in John's account of the washing of the feet (John 13:3-15), Jesus tells the disciples, "You call me Teacher and Lord, and rightly so, for that is what I am. Then if I, your Lord and Teacher, have washed your feet, you also ought to wash one another's feet. I have set you an example: you are to do as I have done for you."

Seen in this light, the biblical command to exercise dominion becomes, for Christians, a command to become servants, to take the lowest place at the (ecological) table. In light of this, Christian readers of Genesis 1:28, far from finding a passage that justifies the abuse and consumption of the rest of creation, must hear a command to exercise the servant leadership of the Son of Man toward the rest of creation. The lordship to be exercised by humans over other creatures is to be modeled not on the dominion of empires but on the stewardship of Israel over the land of Canaan, on the Suffering Servant of Isaiah, and on the lordship of Christ, who did not deem equality with God as something to be grasped at, but instead took the form of a slave to all of creation (Phil 2:6-7).

In Genesis 1:28 humans are placed over other creatures because their special talents and skills allow them to image the Creator and restorer of beauty by serving all of creation, by fostering and protecting the vitality, diversity, and sustainability of communities of life. Gus diZerega makes a similar point when he argues that the unique superiority (or lordship?) of humans is to be found not in their capacity to control, conquer, or dominate other creatures but in their singular ability to empathize with and care about others that are radically different from themselves.[80] In other words, humanity's lordship over other creatures is to be found in their unique ability to recognize, respect, and respond to the intrinsic value and beauty of all other creatures.

CREATED AS GARDENERS

In the second creation narrative of Genesis 2:5-25, humans are also created to tend and care for the beauty of creation. Here, though, they are not created as artists fashioned in the image and likeness of a creator, restorer, and enjoyer of beauty. Instead, they are specifically created as gardeners and placed within Eden to till and look after this botanical paradise. The biblical author of the second creation narrative makes this point three times in the first eleven verses of the story. In Genesis 2:5 we read that before God had sent rain to water the earth or planted any trees or shrubs, there was no one to till the ground, suggesting that such a creature would be needed for the earth's vegetation, and Eden's garden in particular, to grow and blossom. Then in Genesis 2:7-8 we read that God forms the human before planting the garden in Eden and places this living creature in the garden as soon as it is planted, implying that the human is created for this specific purpose, to tend and care for the beauty of Eden. Finally, in Genesis 2:15 we read that "the LORD God took the man and put him in the garden of Eden to till it and look after it."

Indeed, there is some reason to suggest that the author of the second creation narrative sees God as a gardener as well, for the Garden of Eden is clearly the crowning jewel or summit of this creation account, much as the day of rest forms the capstone of the palatial temple constructed in the first creation narrative. In addition, like a gardener, this God has formed all life out of the dust or soil of the earth. Humans have been formed of the dust of the earth and planted in the garden. Every tree

---

[80] DiZerega, "Empathy, Society, Nature," 260.

and shrub God creates in this story is planted in Eden's garden. All rivers flow from the river that waters Eden. And all the planet's wild animals and birds are formed from the soil of this garden.

So in this second creation narrative, humans are fashioned by a gardener God to be gardeners—to till and look after Eden, that vibrant, luxuriously abundant, richly diverse, and lavishly fruitful biotic community that is the source and summit of God's creation. Humans, by their very nature, have been created to tend and care for the living community of creation. This is their divine and ecological calling, revealed in their vocation to be gardeners.

Many suggest that the vocation to be gardeners means humans are to be stewards and caretakers of creation; and this is certainly true. But a gardener is not merely tending crops and grains, husbanding plants and livestock, feeding and restocking animals, watering and tilling the soil. Being a gardener also implies tending and caring for beauty. A gardener needs more than a green thumb. She needs an eye for color, harmony, variety, contrast, and clarity. If the hanging gardens of Babylon, the architectural wonders of Versailles, and the lush greenery of Monet's gardens at Giverny are any indication, gardens are a work of beauty, and gardeners have a calling to care for and tend this beauty.

To be a gardener means caring for, protecting, and fostering the delicate and dynamic balance of animals, plants, and minerals that make up a garden. It means appreciating the wonder and goodness of each living organism and understanding how the dance of all these various creatures can be fostered in a way to create a larger, more dynamic, and more integral beauty. It means being able to recognize and foster all the various talents and gifts of each and every creature in order to orchestrate a vibrant and sustainable masterpiece that will grow, bear fruit, and evolve through the seasons and years.

Like the artist, the gardener is the servant of creation's beauty, drawn in by the indwelling lure of beauty that is the presence of God in the universe. And like the artist, the gardener must imagine, design, restore, and tend to the beauty of creation—and must, of course, delight in this beauty. In addition, however, the gardener is an artist laboring on a living and evolving masterpiece, an artist who recognizes, responds to, and respects the autonomous creativity of the natural world and all its creatures. Working not merely with paint and palette or stone and chisel, the gardener, more like a parent or teacher, must make room for, cooperate with, and even encourage the evolving creativity and fruitfulness of different life forms, as well as their wondrously creative and dynamic interaction with all other living beings and habitats.

In this way the gardener of Genesis 2:5-31 is as far away as possible from the owner and master of chattel and is the polar opposite of the agricultural emperor who exercises dominion by bending all living creatures to his will, subjugating all beings to his control. This gardener knows nothing of empires, monoculture plantations, or factory farms that mass produce commodities and seek to reduce the wonder of creation to a piece of machinery. The lowly gardener of Genesis 2:5-31, fashioned of the very dust of the loamy soil in which God has planted every tree, shrub, and bush and from which God has drawn all the wild animals and birds, is a companion, not a master, to all these creatures. This gardener knows and calls all other living creatures by their proper names, sees their deep-down beauty, and recognizes that they all come from (and return to) the same well-watered ground. This gardener cannot be alone or above and on top of the rest of creation, but must be nurtured by the company of a vibrant, diverse, and fruitful community of living creatures.

The twin creation narratives of Genesis 1–2 each affirm that humans have a fundamental and divine calling to tend and care for the beauty of all creation. In the first creation account humans are fashioned in the image and likeness of a divine artist who responds to the lure of beauty in the midst of a chaotic, confused, and exhausted world by creating a living architectural masterpiece teeming with vitality and diversity. In an age when our own increasingly exhausted and depleted world bears the scars and ravages of pollution, overconsumption, and degradation, it is essential that we remember and recover this God-given vocation to be artists. Meanwhile, in the second creation account humans are fashioned, placed, and commissioned as gardeners of God's living creation, challenging and correcting any tendency we might have to see ourselves as lords and masters or owners of the natural world, and reminding us of our duty to tend and care for the beauty of all creation.

Conclusion

The beauty of nature has been one of the primary motivating forces behind calls for environmental legislation and reform. Perhaps this is because our encounter with beauty tends to unself and decenter us from our narcissistic concerns and routine obsessions in a more joyful and effective manner than does the imposition of ethical duties or the revelation of future catastrophes, which we can experience as a burden, constraint, or threat. Perhaps it is because in our experience of the beauty of nature we recognize its intrinsic value and take delight in it as something wondrous and lovely in its own right. The problem with most traditional aesthetic arguments, however, is that they have focused on a small cluster of creatures and habitats that modern artistic sensibilities find to be strikingly attractive or sublime, ignoring or overlooking the real beauty (and intrinsic worth) of the vast majority of animals, plants, and settings considered to be plain or unattractive. This derivative and self-referential aesthetic approach does not really see the beauty of nature but only recognizes natural creatures and scenes as beautiful when they resemble a charming pet or a stunning landscape painting.

Aldo Leopold attempts to address this shortcoming by developing an autonomous land aesthetic that uncovers the beauty and intrinsic worth of all creatures and habitats. He does this by rejecting the notion that nature is a two-dimensional landscape to be measured by the artistic sensibilities of an external human observer. Instead, Leopold demands we meet nature on its own terms, immersing ourselves in the ecologically diverse, historically evolving, and three-dimensional world of nature and engaging all our senses and our intellect and our imagination to help us recognize, respect, and respond to the intrinsic but overlooked beauty and worth of the whole natural world. In particular, Leopold the naturalist uses the insights of ecological and evolutionary science to uncover the stunning but often unseen diversity, complexity, and dynamic integrity of a savannah or watering hole, or to marvel at the amazing adaptability and fitness of common or even brutish-looking creatures that have survived or flourished through countless millennia of change.

For Leopold, uncovering the beauty of all creation requires a transformation of the human heart and intellect, as well as the development of a land aesthetic that sees the beauty hidden beneath the often plain and common surface of nature. So, while the lure of charming pets and scenic landscapes may begin to awaken humanity's concern for nature, only a love of natural beauty that recognizes the universal beauty of creation will be able to do the heavy ecological lifting before us.

In spite of the ecological complaint long associated with the command of Genesis 1:28 to dominate and subjugate the rest of creation, the two creation narratives of Genesis 1–2 could indeed be seen as offering and advancing the very sort of autonomous land aesthetic presented by Leopold. For in these two narratives the biblical authors repeatedly and persuasively affirm the beauty of all creation and of every creature, a beauty that does not depend in any way upon how useful or attractive they are to humans. At the same time, both narratives consistently reject any separation of humans from the rest of creation; instead, they immerse humanity deeply within the larger masterpiece of the created world. And, finally, both in the affirmation that humans are made in the image and likeness of the artist who creates, restores, and delights in the beauty of creation and in the claim that humans are made to be Eden's gardeners, these narratives establish that it is humanity's deepest calling to care for and tend to the beauty of creation.

Aldo Leopold was convinced that the only way to save the natural world from human indifference and abuse was to awaken the human heart to the unseen and universal beauty of the created world, to humanity's integral place within that world of beauty, and to our human calling to tend and care for all of nature's beauty. Ironically enough, the very biblical narratives that Lynn White and others have blamed for Christianity's indifference to the natural world summon us to recognize, respect, and respond to the beauty of all creation, remind us of humanity's radical immersion in that world of beauty, and recall our fundamental and divine vocation to tend and care for this beauty.

Index